24/7 EMBODYING Christ-like LEADERSHIP

L E S L I E   C O P E L A N D

Foreword by W. Franklyn Richardson

JUDSON PRESS
PUBLISHERS SINCE 1824
VALLEY FORGE, PA

24/7 Embodying Christ-like Leadership
© 2022 by Judson Press, Valley Forge, PA 19482-0851
All rights reserved.

Interior and cover design by Wendy Ronga, Hampton Design Group.

Library of Congress Cataloging-in-Publication data
Cataloging-in-Publication Data available upon request.
Contact cip@judsonpress.com.

Printed in the U.S.A.
First printing, 2022.

CONTENTS

Foreword

I have known Leslie Copeland most of her life. Knowing her has made me proud of her.

As her pastor, I watched her bud and bloom into an exciting teenager, a loyal sister, a devoted daughter, a loving mother, an authentic Christian voice, and an engaging ecumenical leader. I am excited to bear witness to the authenticity of this book's author. She is a critical thinker and a passionate servant of Christ.

On these pages, you will experience her boldness in presenting an honest assessment of the issues confronting Christian leadership today. Rev. Dr. Copeland is critical without condescending and confrontational without arrogance. She brings fresh insight to the abiding challenge of effective leadership in the church and the world. Leslie brings a fresh perspective of what is required of Christian leaders. Her challenging the irrational thinking of leaders during the pandemic is vitally needed. She calls out leadership behaviors that are antithetical to the gospel of Jesus Christ and harmful to people of faith who follow without questioning the rationality of their thinking. This book provides a mirror into which each of us who have leadership responsibilities can see ourselves afresh.

Moreover, this work offers an opportunity for the church to ask the question; "Leadership to where?" What are the Christian mandates that define our forward direction as communities of faith? I think that her voice on these matters from the perspective of a female leader brings fresh critique from those who have been marginalized and denied by those who provide ineffective leadership, bad Bible, and endemic theology. On these pages, she makes a strong case for reimagining Christian leadership based on the mandates of the life and message of the historical Jesus. The Lord is speaking to the church and its leadership, challenging it to greater relevance. Are we listening?

Beyond what I have said is the fact that this book is not narrow in its intended audience. Its relevance is not confined by race, denomination, nor tradition. The wide intended focus of the message contained in this writing flows from the author's expansive career engagement with diverse communities and leaders across denominations. Her ministry has been molded at the intersection of conservative and liberal thought within the ecumenical community. This book has a message for the entire Christian church. I assure you if you approach this reading with openness, the discovery will leave you with fresh reflection on how to be a more effective and faithful leader for the cause of Christ.

Dr. Copeland in this book calls all of us to inculcate the radical model of Jesus if we would lead as we follow him. The concepts put forward on these pages are therapeutic for the novice and the veteran in ministry. It is engaging and encouraging for those who seek to reflect the priorities of Jesus as we lead his people on an unknown path but to a certain destiny.

—Dr. W. Franklyn Richardson
Senior Pastor, Grace Baptist Church,
Mount Vernon, New York
Chair of the Conference of National Black Churches and
Chair of the Board for Virginia Union University

Acknowledgments

I am so grateful for my journey—for the times that I got things right and the times I fell short. I can truly say that God has wasted nothing, and I have been able to incorporate the good and learn from the bad, including both into my leadership and ministry. My faith has fortified and kept me, even through my own doubts and insecurities, and no words can adequately express how grateful I am. *Thank you, Jesus!*

I am profoundly grateful to my mom, Evelyn R. Walker Copeland, who has led by example and been unwavering as the biggest advocate, cheerleader, supporter, and straight-shooter in my life; and, for my dad, John C. Copeland, who has been with the ancestors since 2012 and who always supported and encouraged me. I miss him more than I ever thought I would.

I also thank my sister and best friend, Lisa A. Copeland. There is probably no one who knows me better than my sister. She is always on my side, in my corner, advocating and supporting me. I would not have made it through some of the most difficult moments in my life without her, and I am forever grateful for how God knew before I was born that I would need a sister like her to help me navigate through this life and Christian journey.

This book is dedicated to my young adult children, Aman Victoria and Jordan, who are coming into their own in so many ways and making me proud every day—not just because of what they are doing with their lives but because of who they are as human beings. They have kept me going in challenging moments when I wanted to give up. Truly, they are the epitome of God's grace in my life, and I am thankful for them. They also journeyed with me through writing this book, offering feedback and support along the way.

The idea for this book started with an invitation from Rev. Dr. Amaury Tañón-Santos, who was in my DMin, cohort at New Brunswick Theological Seminary. He invited me to be a speaker at a congregational leaders gathering at a local church in my area for Princeton Theological Seminary. I ended up on a panel with Dr. Adam L. Bond, who asked me to contribute a chapter based on my presentation to a book Rev. Laura Mariko Cheifetz and he were writing, entitled *Church on Purpose: Reinventing Discipleship, Community, and Justice* (Judson Press, 2015). I am grateful for each of them—and how what I thought would be one day of my time has become so much more.

I have been blessed to have wonderful people in my life who have mentored and journeyed with me. I am especially grateful for Revs. Stacey Hamilton, NaShieka Knight, and Charisse R. Tucker, who were my regular sounding boards for this book. I also want to express gratitude for my dearest friends and line sisters Doris Ramseur Davis, who gave me important feedback and suggestions, and Tracy Washington Craig and her son, Marcus, who helped me with research for the book. Rev. Brenda Girton-Mitchell is a friend and mentor who opened numerous doors for me and has provided endless support, advice, and encouragement. A special thanks also goes to Amaya Smith, who is a true sister and friend who has encouraged me to write and supported me through the process. I also give thanks and praise for my Duke Divinity School prayer group, the Proverbs 31 Women, Revs. Margaret Coleman, Della Owens, Gladys Long, and Jocleen McCall. I am especially grateful for Rev. Cheryl Adamson, who shared her insights with me, read parts of the book and gave me feedback. We have been praying with and for each other through life's ups and downs since we walked those halls together, and I am grateful for all of them.

I am grateful to Rev. Dr. Cheryl Price for her support and wisdom, not only for this project but also throughout the years. I am grateful for Rev. Rebecca Irwin-Diehl, who encouraged me to write the book proposal, and Rev. Dr. Rachael Lawrence, who has walked me through this process with care and support. I also want to thank Lisa Blair, Gale Tull, and the entire Judson Press team for their patience, feedback, and encouragement.

A debt of gratitude goes to my family, the Dunbar Walker clan, especially the elders and those now a part of the great cloud of witnesses cheering me on. I particularly want to express appreciation for Michelle Lakins-Waller, who encouraged me, read parts of this work, and took me out to celebrate when I finished the manuscript. I am also grateful for Dana Lakins Peters, Mitea Lakins Cunningham, and Von Harris who gave me much-needed feedback.

I have several sister and clergy circles for which I am profoundly grateful. I am especially grateful to Rev. Dr. W. Franklyn Richardson, who baptized me and has been such a powerful and important influence in my Christian journey as well as my work for justice. You are the best!

For those who have shared their wisdom with me for this project and gave me words of encouragement, a text, and a gentle nudge when I needed it most, I also give thanks, including Rev. Dr. Judy Fentress-Williams, Rev. Traci Blackmon, Rev. Andrea Chambers, Rev. Dr. Cynthia Turner Wood, Rev. Dr. Joy Challenger-Slaughter, Rev. Dr. Barbara Williams-Skinner, Rev. Dawn Sanders, Rev. Aundreia Alexander, Debra A. Shaw, Cynthia Cotte Griffiths, Rev. Essentino Lewis, Rev. Courtenay L. Miller, Rev. Michael Livingston, Rev. Dr. Jean Luc Charles, and, Rev. Charles (Chuck), Jr., and Bethany Dickerson Wynder. I extend a special thanks to Rev. Dr. Howard-John Wesley and my Alfred Street Baptist Church family.

To Rev. Dr. Chanequa Walker-Barnes and Rev. Jonathan Wilson-Hartgrove, who facilitated my writing retreat at Collegeville

Institute, as well as to my entire cohort of mystic activist writers—you helped me to embrace being a writer in a deeper way, and I am grateful.

To my sorors of Delta Sigma Theta Sorority, Inc., most especially to my line sisters, and Sorors of Kappa Lambda chapter—I am grateful for you seeing something in me that I did not see in myself. You asked me to lead when I was not at all sure I knew what I was doing, and you supported me along the way. It meant a lot then, and your continued support means a lot now.

I appreciate so many people who have shown me by example what it means to be a leader—especially an effective Christian leader. Although there are too many to name specifically, I must acknowledge the late Bishop Thomas L. Hoyt and the late Rev. Dr. Faye Gunn.

Someone once told me that a large part of my ministry would be writing. At the time, I did not take this as a compliment. Coming from a Black Baptist tradition where preaching is centered, I could not help but wonder if he was trying to steer me away from the pulpit. I knew he was not slighting me, but I also did not know how to process what it meant to have a writing ministry. I now know that he was planting a seed that would be watered throughout my journey, and God would ultimately give the increase. Thank you, Rev. Dr. Kelvin Turner for speaking into my life despite my resistance to what was being said.

He was not alone. Many have encouraged, nudged, supported, loved, and tolerated me along the way. With a grateful heart and deep appreciation, I say thank you!

Introduction

So, You Want to Be a Christian Leader?

"It is not enough for the priests and ministers of the future to be moral people, well trained, eager to help their fellow humans, and able to respond creatively to the burning issues of their time. All of that is very valuable and important, but it's not the heart of Christian leadership. The central question is, Are the leaders of the future truly men and women of God, people with an ardent desire to dwell in God's presence, to listen to God's voice, to look at God's beauty, to touch God's incarnate Word and to taste fully God's infinite goodness?" —Henri J.M. Nouwen[1]

"So let us not grow weary in doing what is right, for we will reap at harvest time, if we do not give up. So then, whenever we have an opportunity, let us work for the good of all, and especially for those of the family of faith." —Galatians 6:9-10

Bad leadership can kill. If we have learned nothing from the coronavirus pandemic, it is that having capable leadership is critically important. This is especially true when a racial justice uprising and economic crisis coincide with a pandemic and a nation's cultural norms are put on public display for critique and dissection.

A lack of national leadership to end the devastating impacts of the virus and address the issues of systemic racism boiled over into the streets and left this nation teetering on the edge of what might be an implosion.

Unfortunately, the church as a whole has not modeled the kind of leadership that would make a difference when it has been so desperately needed. Instead of filling in the gaps from the dearth of national leadership, churches have been woefully divided on how to bring justice, healing, and hope to a nation in crisis. Some faith leaders urged people not to take simple precautions to safeguard themselves from an airborne virus, such as wearing masks or getting vaccinated, by assuring them that God would protect them. Others made a false dichotomy between believing in science and trusting God. In this way, some presumedly well-intentioned church leaders weaponized theology placing people in harm's way. They manipulated godly hope and confused it with wishful thinking as it related to both the pandemic and its economic impacts as well as to the epidemic of racism in this country. Church worship services and funeral services, as well as other activities, were some of the catalysts for exponential spreading of the coronavirus. Some pastors erroneously equated attending church in a building with having a mature faith, even though that decision put the lives of many parishioners at risk. Bad leadership can kill.

We have numerous examples of pastors and other church leaders who made tough decisions to protect the lives of those in their congregations. They expanded their food pantries and benevolence ministries to meet the growing needs of their communities. They began difficult conversations on racism and engaged in the hard work of ending injustice. They shepherded their congregations in ways that have allowed them to grow and survive these trying circumstances. Good, sound leadership makes a difference and helps people thrive.

What makes the difference? For Christians, leadership is not something to take off and put on like the latest social justice T-shirt, button, or hat. Christ-like leadership is to permeate our lives. We should *be leaders*, not simply do leadership.

In this book, I define leadership as the ways by which a person influences others using their skills, abilities, personality, and resources to inspire growth, cast vision, lay the groundwork, and pave the way for others to achieve shared goals and objectives. These shared goals and objectives help individuals, churches, faith-based organizations, corporations, and non-profits, as well as other entities, to prosper and realize their God-given purpose and potential. The characteristics outlined in each of my chapters are a way for Christians to embody Christ-like leadership—all day, every day, 24/7.

Unfortunately, most people in our nation have for years believed that there are not enough effective leaders, Christian or otherwise. A study on leadership conducted by Barna Research in 2013 showed that 82 percent of people who describe themselves as Christians believe there is a crisis in our country because we don't have enough good examples of leaders in the United States.[2] Perhaps more concerning is that many of the character traits identified as important for leaders were not qualities that those who identified themselves as leaders believed they exhibited. Another Barna study of young adults conducted in partnership with World Vision in 2019 found that 82 percent of survey respondents believe that "society is facing a crisis of leadership because there are not enough good leaders right now."[3] Surprisingly, about 30 percent of young adults believe that they are not now, nor have they ever been, leaders. These are disturbing trends. They present an opportunity for us to reimagine Christian leadership.

Recent crises in our nation have shown that it takes more than a list of dos and don'ts to be a good leader. Knowing the "right" thing to do or say at any given moment does not equate to good leadership in every situation. There is something different about authentic leadership that carries people, churches, organizations, and corporations through the most difficult and challenging times. Certainly, it's one thing for a person to do leadership tasks that help move an organization in a positive direction. It is quite another to embody leadership, to *be* a leader, in such a way that people within an organization can move together in a positive direction. And let's face it—most people can tell when someone is faking it.

Time and time again, scenarios with poor leadership at the forefront make headlines and give us cause for great concern. When it comes to the church and congregational life, the mistakes and stumbling blocks are endless, too often resulting in church splits and parishioners left hurt by the place that was supposed to provide healing and hope. We expect the church to be a refuge, but poor leadership can make it dreadful.

When I began closely examining what it means to be a Christian leader—to embody Christian leadership—I had to consider the complexities and nuances that are involved when we talk about the church and leadership.[4] The truth is, the church is messy. And church leadership is sometimes a "hot mess." From pastors and other church leaders who steal money and engage in sexually immoral behaviors, to those who flaunt overly extravagant lifestyles and participate in ill-advised programs and activities— having the words *Christian* and *leadership* together can sometimes appear to be a contradiction. It's not that we necessarily start out trying to make a mess of things, but more often than we care to admit, as Christian leaders our best efforts at leading sometimes end in organized disaster and controlled chaos. Not to mention that sometimes we hurt those we aim to help and leave people wounded and running away from, not toward, the church. Indeed, Christian leaders are called to live lives in a paradoxical tension of oxymoronic behavior that makes our leadership efforts more difficult than they might be for others.

We are called out and set apart yet called to be in the midst, rolling up our sleeves, getting our hands dirty, and journeying with others.

We are to be united and to show in miraculous and supernatural ways unity in the body of Christ, yet we are constantly and consistently divided. We are supposed to be set apart, but too often we represent the status quo. In addition, we are to lead as followers, direct people as servants, and point to perfection knowing that we are disastrously imperfect. We follow the one whose death gave us new life and whose life causes us to die daily! We live in paradoxical tension. At its very core, Christian leadership requires us to negotiate a treacherous terrain and exhibit oxymoronic behavior. This reality for Christian believers is coupled with the duplicitous nature of being in the world but not of the world, of becoming all things to gain one, of pointing to perfection when we are flawed.

If we are not careful, we can become like the Pharisees, Sadducees, and scribes, who resisted and opposed Jesus at every turn with their religiosity and sanctimonious attitudes. On the other end of the spectrum, we can become "practical atheists,"[5] saying we believe in God but lack in faith, zeal, and knowledge when it comes to the church and the things of God. But there is a balance between these two ends of the spectrum. Certainly, with all the many challenges facing the church, not the least of which is declining numbers in both membership and participation, leadership may not seem to be the most pressing issue. If church members are few, what difference does it make who is leading? Some would say marketing is the biggest issue; others argue it's the organizational structure and rigidity that's the problem. I've even heard that some of the younger generations complain that mid-morning on a Sunday is not a convenient time for church service since it conflicts with brunch and other fun activities.

Despite the speculation about what is wrong with the church, I suggest that having a cadre of sound and dedicated leaders is at the heart of a reinvigorated and reinvented church. If the church is going to be relevant for future generations, having well-prepared and faithful followers of Christ plotting the course for local congregations and Christian-led organizations is essential. We need a core group of leaders who are committed to the work of the church and who have a keen understanding of both "from whence we came" and where we are trying to go. I further suggest that these Christian leaders should embody leadership in whatever context they find themselves, both inside and outside the walls of the church. These Christian leaders must be able to translate current-day realities through the lens of the gospel and be willing and able to proclaim a living Savior to a dying world, even as they bear fruit that shows the transformative power of the Holy Spirit working in and through us. They have to understand the world but not be controlled by it. They must be Christian leaders who are not so intrigued by the world that they conform to it; nor can they be so opposed to the world that they are not able to minister to those in it. In other words, these Christians cannot be, as Oliver Wendell Holmes, Sr. famously said, "... so heavenly minded that they are of no earthly good."

How then can Christians in a modern context approach leadership in a balanced and authentic way that reinvigorates the church and moves God's people forward to advance God's kingdom on earth? I suggest that there are several foundational principles for reimagining Christian leadership in a way that goes beyond starting meetings on time and keeping them short. These principles will help us to meet the challenges of the day, develop faithful leaders, and draw others to Christ and to the church while being a welcome presence in the community and the world in which we live.

This book comes at a time during which we have experienced the deadly and traumatic results of poor leadership—both in the church and in secular society. We've seen that bad leadership can kill and cause immeasurable harm, while good leadership can propel us to not only survive but to prosper.

In addition, we need to recognize that in our current environment the church is woefully divided. Saying that we are not all on the same page when it comes to Christian leadership in our nation is a profound understatement. The way in which our Christian witness has been compromised in the tug-of-war over the social issues of our times is stark and appalling. It will take dedicated Christian leaders who are willing to fully embrace the call to be ambassadors and repairers of the breach to move us to a healthier place. It will also take some soul-searching, truth-telling, and agape love to help us forge the way ahead. It is my hope that *24/7 Embodying Christ-like Leadership* will be a tool that equips Christian leaders as we embark on this journey together.

I believe that the character traits of Christian leaders that I identify in this book are the most important aspects of Christian leadership. People can lead regardless of their faith tradition or absence thereof. But authentic Christian leadership must have a grounding in faith that is reflective of the "new creation" we become in Christ as believers. I am not at all suggesting that Christian leaders have to be close to perfect. However, effective Christian leaders exhibit visible evidence of leadership that distinguishes them from others. Galatians 5:22-26 details for us the evidence that we are living by the Spirit. We are told that joy, peace, patience, kindness, generosity, faithfulness, gentleness, and self-control are all fruit of the Spirit and indicators that the Spirit is not only dwelling in us but leading us.

While this book presents a different set of categories to offer a standard for Christian leadership, the fruit of the Spirit are an implicit part of these characteristics, which include call, Christ, clarity, character, courage, conviction, commitment, compassion, care, credibility, consequences of bad leadership, and cultivating Christian leadership. These are all foundational principles on which Christian leaders must be able to stand as well as epitomize. None of these characteristics alone would make someone a good Christian leader. Yet, as a cohesive part of the leadership style, personality, and behavior of a Christian leader, these characteristics have the potential to move the church and God's people in a positive, wholesome, and healthy direction. Certainly, these characteristics should work in concert, not competing against or in conflict with one another. *24/7 Embodying Christ-like Leadership* is not offering a formula for Christian leadership so much as identifying necessary components for being a Christian leader who can positively impact and influence people, change lives, and transform communities, all to God's glory.

In describing the characteristics in this book that exemplify authentic Christian leadership, I use words that I believe encapsulate concepts and foundational principles. There is no rationale for using alliteration with all *C* words. It's just where I found inspiration and cohesiveness. Some of the characteristics also are obvious, such as call, character, and courage. Others may not be quite as apparent, including clarity, care, and conviction. Yet, these all work together in molding, shaping, and cultivating someone to be a Christian leader and not simply doing leadership activities.

A great deal has been said about leadership, and by some of the best and most prolific writers of our times. Authors like John Maxwell and Henri Nouwen, as well as many others, have all written about leadership. Maxwell is a world-renowned and bestselling author of books on leadership. In many ways, he has saturated the leadership market with books that have Christian-themed principles of leadership without being explicitly Christian. This is not a criticism of Maxwell's approach; rather, it is an observation that this book offers a different approach to what is currently available in books on Christian leadership. Similarly, Nouwen, who was (and still is) a highly regarded theologian and author, addresses complementing themes in his books on leadership. In general, Nouwen is interested in the spiritual disciplines and inward life that ministers should practice. Nouwen's book *In the Name of Jesus: Reflections on Christian Leadership* contends that leadership is not just about the individual but also about the community. This is true on multiple levels.[6]

Leaders bears responsibility for the people whom they lead and the impact their leadership has on those around them. Yet, Nouwen focuses his book on aspects of ministry that leaders should be aware of, with each chapter dealing with the temptation and discipline for leaders in various areas of their lives as well as issues they must address in their ministries. This book doesn't negate or replace the work of Maxwell and Nouwen. Instead, *24/7 Embodying Christ-like Leadership* is casting a vision for how Christian leadership should be viewed, embraced, and manifested both inside and outside the walls of the church.

Another informative work that is not specifically about Christian leadership but delves into similar leadership principles is Marvin McMickle's *The Making of a Preacher: 5 Essentials for Ministers Today*. In this work, McMickle focuses on preachers, who are in most cases the primary leaders in churches. His roadmap for preachers contains similar character traits as this book, such as call, character, and consequences. His work is referenced in those chapters to demonstrate some of the nuances of Christian leadership and how the principles that apply to ministers are instructive for those who are Christian leaders in other roles.[7]

This book adds to the thinking about Christian leadership, positioning characteristics that make a leader—a decidedly *Christian* leader. My hope is that this book will push us to embody Christian leadership regardless of the setting. This seems to be particularly critical as we negotiate the times in which we live. Perhaps that has been true in every time period, but it seems particularly poignant now. Since the onset of the coronavirus pandemic, church has been happening in ways we never anticipated. Life is happening in ways we hadn't expected. In real and profound ways, we have had to recognize that we don't know what we don't know. Good leadership is always needed as we navigate through the ups and downs of life. For the church, being intentional about how we build up and become Christian leaders is critical as we rebuild a nation and world torn and tattered by conflict, chaos, confusion, and divisiveness.

The foundational principles in this book do not by any means detract from the work of the Spirit to lead us, guide us, mold us, and shape us into the likeness of Christ. Note, we sometimes learn the best lessons by failing. Every once in a while, God teaches us and shows us the most about leadership when we get it wrong. Some have referred to this as the *refiner's fire*; others call it learning from our mistakes. Life is messy and leadership can be more so. Sometimes even with the best guidelines and parameters and with the wisest counsel and insights offered to us, experience helps us to grow into the people God purposed us to be. Still, it is helpful to have guideposts and signs along the journey. *24/7 Embodying Christ-like Leadership* seeks to be just that—and to push us to think more broadly and deeply about what it means to be a successful Christian leader in the truest sense of the word.

Notes

1. Henri J.M. Nouwen, *In the Name of Jesus: Reflections on Christian Leadership* (New York: Crossroad Publishing, 1993).

2. "Christians on Leadership, Calling and Career," Barna Research, accessed October 22, 2020, https://www.barna.com/research/christians-on-leadership-calling-and-career/.

3. "82% of Young Adults Say Society Is in a Leadership Crisis," Barna Research, accessed October 22, 2020, https://www.barna.com/research/leadership-crisis/.

4. The content for this was originally developed and published in *Church on Purpose: Reinventing Discipleship, Community & Justice,* edited by Adam L. Bond and Laura Mariko Cheifetz (Valley Forge, PA: Judson Press, 2015).

5. I first heard the term "practical atheist" used in relation to the work of Dr. Stanley Hauerwas, a professor of Christian Ethics, when I was a student at Duke Divinity School.

6. Nouwen, *In the Name of Jesus.*

7. Marvin A. McMickle, *The Making of a Preacher: 5 Essentials for Ministers Today* (Valley Forge, PA: Judson Press, 2018).

CHAPTER 1

Call: It's Not about You

"Lord, I'm going to hold steady on to you and you've got to see me through." —Harriet Tubman[1]

"For we are God's handiwork, created in Christ Jesus to do good works, which God prepared in advance for us to do." —Ephesians 2:10, NIV

"For we are what he has made us, created in Christ Jesus for good works, which God prepared beforehand to be our way of life." —Ephesians 2:10

Harriet Tubman is one of the most well-known and remarkable Christian leaders in American history. She escaped the horrors of slavery and then led hundreds of enslaved people to freedom through the Underground Railroad—a network of abolitionists and safe houses that led those escaping slavery out of harm's way. For this, she was called the "Black Moses." She was also a leader in the Union Army and the first woman to lead an armed expedition in the Civil War. After the war, she transformed from an abolitionist to a political activist who continued the fight for justice until her death. Her courage and bravery came out of a sense of call. She believed that God led her to free God's people from the bondage of slavery. In a 2019 movie adaptation of her life, Tubman tells her former slave owner, "God don't mean people to own people, Gideon!" She understood that slavery was a sin and that her call and mission were to free her people from it. Her simple prayer was this: "Lord, I'm going to hold steady on to You and You've got to see me through." She trusted that God would help her navigate the road to freedom and lead her through dangers seen and unseen, treacherous terrain, inclement weather, dogs who tracked her, and mobs who sought to capture her. Records show that she led the people as she followed God. That's Christian leadership!

But Sam Bowers believed he was called by God, too. According to Charles Marsh, Bowers instituted a four-year campaign of terrorism during which he was suspected of orchestrating at least nine murders; seventy-five bombings of Black churches; and three hundred assaults, bombings, and beatings.[2] After a troubled childhood, he entered the U.S. Navy and found a sense of purpose. He fought in World War II against the Nazis and celebrated when the Allies won. However, upon being discharged, Bowers felt lost and helpless, and almost committed suicide. He didn't really have any friends, and those closest to him were distant because of his anger issues. He began reading Nazi literature and racist philosophies, including Thomas Dixon novels *The Leopard's Spots* and *The Clansmen* (this book was the basis for the racist movie *Birth of a Nation*). He wore a swastika armband and reportedly would click his heels in front of his dog, saluting him with "Heil Hitler."[3]

At the moment he was ready to take his own life, he believed he heard God's voice telling him, "Don't be afraid; everything is all right."[4] He began to earnestly study Scripture and felt connected to the prophets and the apostle Paul. He started to believe that his rage and anger, which he had dealt with his entire life, could be put to service for the "work of the Lord." What Bowers believed was his personal Damascus-Road conversion experience resulted in a belief that God had called him for a divine purpose—to terrorize and kill Black people and anyone involved in the Civil Rights Movement.

Marsh writes that Bowers believed that "no one less than Jesus Christ himself was calling him to the priestly task of preserving the purity of his blood and soil."[5] Bowers started the White Knights of the Ku Klux Klan of Mississippi, which grew to six thousand members and wreaked havoc on the town of Laurel, Mississippi, and the surrounding areas. He was reckless and arrogant, was eventually sentenced to prison for ten years, and then returned to Laurel after serving time, where, ironically, he ended up living in a Black community. A leader? Arguably, yes. A Christian leader? Hardly.

Two people who identify as Christians. Two who believed God called them to lead their people. Two different realities in how their call was understood, lived out, and manifested in their lives and the lives of those around them. Harriet Tubman put her life on the line to set others free from slavery, while Sam Bowers used members of his group to inflict pain on and terrorize Black people and their White allies. The stark differences in these two stories are a cautionary tale but also exemplify the points that (1) understanding one's call and who does the calling is absolutely crucial to Christian leadership, (2) a call into leadership is a call to serve, not to be served, (3) the agenda and mission are God's, not ours, and (4) God's call is consistent with God's character and purpose, which does not include terrorizing, harassing, abusing, nor killing people. That's just not how God works. It is important to recognize that there are places in Scripture where killing seems to be sanctioned, where there appears to be a direct correlation between God's calling and violence ensuing. There is no simple answer or explanation for these passages. They have their own contexts, which require deeper analysis than the goals of this book. Suffice it to say that whether it's "thou shalt not kill" (Exodus 20:13, KJV) or "love your neighbor as yourself" (Matthew 22:39) or other instructions about living in community with others, God's commandments and the teachings of Jesus overwhelmingly suggest that killing other people is contrary to God's will and is a sin against God.

Why even bring this up? Surely, this chapter could have started with just the reminder about the greatness of Harriet Tubman or some other inspiring narrative about call that left us with a warm and fuzzy feeling. Certainly, we didn't have to be reminded of the ugliness of horrific acts by people who claim to share our faith but believe that God told them to terrorize and kill people. Unfortunately, we must face this reality: discernment of God's voice and call on our lives should be taken seriously and handled with care. While it is true that we *can* properly discern our call, it is also true that it is possible for us to *incorrectly conclude* what we think God is calling us to do. This potential misjudgment is why we always try to be disciplined in our discernment process and humble enough to accept that we could be wrong, or misguided, or misinformed. Or we could have blind spots—places that, because of our background, experiences, or proclivities, make it harder for us to recognize certain pitfalls. None of us is an island unto ourselves; we are part of a much bigger, unfolding story of God's love for God's people. The beauty and wonder of experiencing a call should be held in tension with the gravity of being set apart for the work God has specifically entrusted to us.

One example of how this tension can play out happened on what seemed like a normal Sunday. After the service, a very excited deacon brought a visitor over to me who wanted to know more about what it means to "hear from God," a term I had used in my sermon that day. I began to explain to the young man what it meant and how to discern God's voice. In my explanation, I happened to say something to the effect of "God's voice is always consistent with God's Word. For example, God would never tell you to kill anyone." He told me that he had been hearing voices lately and they were telling him to kill people.

I remained calm during this exchange, but the pastor noticed that something was not quite right. He invited us to his office, and the pastor asked the young man what was going on. He listened to his story and asked the young man how long it had been since he had stopped taking his medication. The young man said, "A few weeks." The pastor advised him to see his doctor, go back on his medication, and then come back to further discuss and embark on his spiritual journey. It was an eye-opening exchange for me! This conversation became a ministry lesson that reminds me not to miss something obvious just because I am looking for a deeper, more spiritual significance. These are not always mutually exclusive, but it is important to be aware that sometimes people's problems can present themselves as spiritual issues when, in fact, they are not.

When people are discerning what God is calling them to do, it is important for those helping them in the discernment process to be sensitive to other issues the person may be dealing with, as well as to ask probing and forthright questions. Being aware of signs of spiritual growth and maturity demonstrated by congregants is also important for church leaders. Too often, the church gets so excited about a person's call, particularly a call to ministry as a vocation, that we don't take the time to help that person navigate the discernment process or equip them with what's needed for the next steps. These steps are critical in helping Christian leaders become grounded enough to faithfully pursue and walk in their calling and to lead in whatever ways they are afforded opportunities to do so.

But what is a *call*?

Understanding the concept of call is critically important for the church as a whole and for the individual. The call is a foundational building block for fortified, effective, and faithful Christian leaders. The call to Christian leadership comes from the Creator of the universe. The church has generally understood call as being something only experienced by those who consider ministry as their primary vocation, even if it is not their primary source of income. However, call really has a much broader meaning and significance. A call is God's way of saying there is something in us—something that God has deposited—and it is time for it to come out. Some of what has been deposited in us is needed for the upbuilding of God's kingdom. The call is something tied to who we are created to be.

What is your passion? What are your gifts? They all have something to do with God's call and the deposit that was made in us. God's deposit, made into the depths of our souls and our beings, is manifested in how we serve and minister to others. As Ephesians 2:10 says, "For we are God's workmanship, created in Christ Jesus to do good works, which God prepared in advance for us to do" (NIV). In the New Revised Standard Version, this same verse is translated, "For we are what he has made us, created in Christ Jesus for good works, *which God prepared beforehand to be our way of life*" (emphasis added). In real and tangible ways, Christian leadership is a way of life—a way of being revealed by what we do as we lead others.

In *The Making of a Preacher: 5 Essentials for Ministers Today*, Marvin A. McMickle describes call as "the inward assurance that by whatever means or method, a person has become absolutely convinced that being a preacher is the work to which God has summoned them."[6] This definition, I believe, also applies to others who are Christian leaders and underscores the significance of what it means to discover and live out one's call. A call to be a leader, no matter the title, is a call to serve God's people. It is not a call to be served by others but to use our gifts, talents, skills, and resources to be God's ambassadors in the world. Knowing, understanding, acknowledging, and accepting what we have been called to do is an integral part of being a resilient, faithful, and effective Christian leader. Both versions of this verse in Ephesians encapsulate the essence of God's call. We are God's handiwork. We are what God has made us. We have been created in Christ Jesus to do *good* works. The work that we have been created to do was prepared in advance for us to do. It is our way of life. Purpose. Plan. God's call.

Different understandings of God's call, as demonstrated in the lives of Harriet Tubman and Sam Bowers, also amplify the fact that call, and discerning of call, is to be done within a community. Discernment should take place with the support and backing of a church or denominational body, as well as with accredited educational training. Many churches and denominations recommend divinity school or seminary as a requirement for ordination. However, formal education is not possible for everyone. In this case, classes at reputable conferences or through denominational bodies are normally more flexible and affordable, as well as highly recommended. The move for schools to offer more online classes also provides an opportunity for theological and leadership training. Acquiring some training beyond Bible study, Sunday school, or Vacation Bible School is essential to equip Christian leaders with the tools they need to serve. Additional training helps to broaden a leader's perspective about ministering to and leading God's people regardless of the setting. Taking advantage of such opportunities is an important part of preparing and operating as a Christian leader.

Many denominations now require counseling as part of the ordination process—a welcome addition, ensuring that ministers are mentally and spiritually healthy before putting them in charge of caring for the needs of their congregants. Certainly, discerning one's call should not be done in a vacuum, where the loudest (and perhaps only) voice is that of the person attempting to discern his or her call.

A word about discernment—it is hard, deliberative work, but it is key to understanding call as well as knowing the next steps to take as a Christian leader. Oftentimes, churches will use spiritual gifts inventories to help parishioners discover their purpose and to identify the areas of ministry in which they are most gifted. While these tools are not perfect, many do offer some guidance as to what ministry focus coincides with the person's passions, gifts, interests, skills, and talents. Spiritual gifts inventories are primarily based on the gifts listed in 1 Corinthians 12 and 14 and Romans 12:4-8. For most, the results are rarely a surprise, as they often confirm what they have experienced and what others have witnessed. Sometimes, a spiritual gifts inventory can reveal a call that a person has been wrestling with and struggling to embrace. Alternatively, such inventories can also reveal areas that are not a person's gifting. For example, the person who has a low score for the gift of hospitality probably should not serve on the usher board. It is important for the results of a spiritual gifts inventory to be discussed and reviewed to better understand what the assessment reveals and the next steps a person might consider taking.

Not every tradition looks at call the same way. In my Baptist tradition, for the most part, the call is understood to be similar to Samuel's encounter with God in 1 Samuel 3. In this text, Samuel hears a voice calling his name and thinks it is the prophet Eli, who has charge over him. After the third time he hears his name, Samuel follows Eli's advice and says, "Speak, for your servant is listening" (1 Samuel 3:10). Here, we see that there is a call and confirmation of the call. An elder is offering guidance and discerns that what Samuel is hearing is the voice of the Lord calling him to serve. This is not the only text that walks us through someone's call and acceptance of the call. Moses has a burning bush. Isaiah sees the Lord high and lifted up and says, "Here am I, send me." Esther has Mordecai. Mary has the angel Gabriel. Paul has the road to Damascus. The disciples have Jesus telling them to follow him. Scripture shows that a call can happen in any number of ways, and no one's call experience is the same, nor should it be. Our call stories are tailor-made by the One who created, molded, and shaped us. Call aligns with our experiences, purpose, and personalities. It is unique to us, as we are unique to God.

For Christian leaders, the importance of having some understanding of call or God's leading cannot be emphasized enough. Taking on the responsibility of leading God's people is a weighty one. Proceeding with both caution and confidence is important to being able to serve faithfully. Nothing is wrong with pursuing further education without having a sense of call, and some people who do not readily recognize their call are sometimes unknowingly following God's direction. However, to pursue Christian leadership roles for selfish reasons, or because it seems like the best option at the time, makes it hard to remain grounded. When leaders are ungrounded, they are more easily swayed by secular models of leadership and ensnared by pitfalls that might otherwise be avoided.

The specificity of an individual's call is not always clear at first. Nobody provides a step-by-step set of instructions when we accept our call. Instead, it is a walk of faith that emerges as time, circumstances, gifts, skills, talents, and opportunities coalesce. Endeavoring to understand our call is part of our work and spiritual journey. Call leads to a sense of purpose, fulfillment, and flourishing. It leads to contentment and steers us to lead in ways that can make a positive and transformative difference in the lives of those we are leading. No one else can accept another person's call for them or compel them to answer a call they may be discerning. Doing so can be disastrous for both parties. Another person can only confirm and affirm; no one can do someone else's spiritual work for them in discovering what they are called to do. McMickle offers this analogy in comparing one's sense of call and their ability to remain engaged in the frequently challenging work of ministry: "The one thing that may allow persons to remain in ministry when they feel like giving up is their deep sense of being called by God to do this work."[7]

Undoubtedly, call is an important part of Christian leadership. Christian leaders should have some sense of being led by God and an understanding that God called them to the work they are doing. This understanding of being called helps to diminish our egos and establishes a sense of accountability. Our accountability is rooted in recognizing that we are doing our work *for the Lord*. Our work is an act of faithfulness to the one who has called us and set us apart. In other words, we need to understand that we are responding to *God's call* in the work in which we are engaged. It's not about us! We are simply earthen vessels being used by God to accomplish God's purposes. This knowledge about call also fuels and energizes us for the work ahead.

Understanding and operating in one's call opens us to God's leading the way and lighting our path. Proverbs 29:18 tells us that without vision the people perish. It is also true that without vision, leaders cannot properly lead. That is why the prophet Habakkuk records God's instruction to write the vision and make it plain. It is especially difficult to know which way to go on a path that you're not supposed to be on in the first place. Our call helps us to discern the vision for leading the people based on the context and circumstances in which we have been assigned to lead.

How our call is lived out can change and evolve (and often does) as we journey with God. Someone may start out pastoring a church and end up in denominational leadership or heading a faith-based organization. The reverse is also true. We as Christian leaders are confident of our call, but also flexible and led by the Spirit to recognize where and in what context we are to lead in different seasons of our lives.

Understanding our call propels us and makes us better Christian leaders, but too often, we encounter those who operate outside of their areas of calling and gifting. Christian leaders who are in positions that do not reflect their callings can have very trying and exasperating experiences. While being outside of our comfort zones can at times lead to spiritual growth, maturity, and personal development, when we are operating within our call, we are most content and fulfilled. The results of not using one's gifts and calling can be discouraging—and a challenge for both the person leading and those they are attempting to lead.

Numerous ministries have declined because the person leading them was not called or well-suited for the position. Moreover, countless examples exist of the person on the mission field who would rather be in a local church or vice versa. When we are operating outside of our lane, so to speak, we are less patient with others, tire more easily, are less creative, and feel less confident. Such situations make the challenging work of leading even more difficult and affect all those who work with us, negatively impacting our collective ministry efforts. Learning to adjust to circumstances beyond our control and to be flexible when assigned an undesirable task helps us to be effective Christian leaders. Of course, in those circumstances, we can pray to God for the grace to endure, thrive, and navigate unfamiliar territory. However, embodying Christ-like leadership also means being very intentional in matching people's assignments and ministry undertakings with their calling to avoid chaos and confusion from emerging.

A few years ago, I was given the opportunity to present a paper at a conference in Brazil based on my doctoral thesis on domestic violence. I was thrilled and couldn't wait to travel to that part of the world. On my way there, I had several travel mishaps, including my luggage being left behind in Washington, DC. My flight was delayed by a total of twelve hours, and I arrived only to find out that my presentation was scheduled first thing the next morning. However, my clothes would not arrive until the next day (if I was lucky). To add to my frustration, although our bathroom was indoors, we could not put any kind of paper in the toilet! I realized in that moment what I had probably already known: while I could find joy in doing missions work, I was not called to be a missionary.

I was irritated and felt like a fish out of water for the first few days of the trip. My good sister-friend and roommate during the trip, on the other hand, took everything in stride. She had been on numerous mission trips and dealt with much worse conditions than our relatively pleasant, albeit simple, surroundings. I began to watch her seemingly effortless handling of the mishaps and obstacles we encountered. She was content, while I was working very hard not to be a negative influence or complainer. After all, there was so much to be grateful for in the experience. In the end, I had a meaningful trip and learned more about myself from having participated. But I also made notes on how to avoid certain situations in the future to every extent possible! One of the takeaways for me was that when operating outside of your area of gifting, the best leadership decision can be to *follow* rather than to try to lead.

In ministry (and in life), having a clear sense of call is imperative. Clarity of call undergirds the determination and steadfastness needed to live out that call. For most Christian leaders, the journey is filled with ups and downs. Sometimes, to withstand the tumultuous landscape of Christian leadership, we must hold on to God and be led as God leads, just like Harriet Tubman. Without a sense of call and purpose—an assurance that this is who God called you to be and what God called you to do—it is hard to be an effective Christian leader in any sustainable way. Without a sense of call and purpose, burnout is more likely. Without a sense of call and purpose, we spin our wheels and end up frustrated, even as we frustrate the people around us. On the other hand, having a sense of call and purpose firmly grounds us, equips us, and strengthens us to do the work that God has called us to do. A call is the foundation on which we stand and upon which we are able to build a lasting hope.

Notes

1. Sarah H. Bradford, *Scenes in the Life of Harriet Tubman* (Independently Published, 2018).

2. Charles Marsh, "High Priest of the Anti-Civil Rights Movement: The Calling of Sam Bowers," in *God's Long Summer: Stories of Faith and Civil Rights* (Princeton: Princeton University Press, 1999), 49.

3. Marsh, 53.

4. Marsh, 54.

5. Marsh, 55.

6. Marvin A. McMickle, *The Making of a Preacher: 5 Essentials for Ministers Today* (Valley Forge, PA: Judson Press, 2018), 7.

7. McMickle, 18.

Christ: Getting Our Jesus Right

"You got to get your Jesus right." —Rev. Dr. Howard-John Wesley, Senior Minister, Alfred Street Baptist Church, Alexandria, Virginia

"You know that the rulers of the Gentiles lord it over them, and their great ones are tyrants over them. It will not be so among you; but whoever wishes to be great among you must be your servant." —Matthew 20:25-26

"Remember your leaders, those who spoke the word of God to you; consider the outcome of their way of life, and imitate their faith. Jesus Christ is the same yesterday and today and forever." —Hebrews 13:7-8

The most important principle for Christian leaders, upon which every other principle depends, is that the individual be a follower of Christ. It may seem obvious, even elementary, but anyone who would serve effectively as a *Christian* leader must believe in the birth, life, death, burial, resurrection, and return of Jesus Christ as the Savior of the world. This belief stands on the assurance that

Jesus Christ died for our sins so that we might be reconciled to God and have eternal life. Many experts on leadership can offer advice and a checklist of guidelines to be an effective leader. But for the person to be a *Christian* leader and faithful servant, belief in Jesus Christ is paramount.

I am a Jesus person. What I mean by that is my faith and *my experience of my faith* is centered on Jesus Christ. Specifically, I believe that Jesus Christ is my Lord and Savior. I believe that he gave his life so that I might live. Jesus' sacrificial act of dying on a cross has paid a debt I could not pay, washed away my sins, and reconciled me back to God. My belief in this atonement is central to my understanding of how the violence of sin and the breach that separated humanity from God can be repaired only through the Lamb of God, namely Jesus Christ. The law could not save us, nor could the judges or the prophets. It was Christ and Christ alone.

I recognize that some within my faith tradition understand atonement theology differently and would disagree with my beliefs. My point here is to share my understanding and how I believe it relates to being a Christian leader. I understand myself to be a disciple of Christ. As such, I hope my thoughts, actions, vocation, work, volunteer efforts, and how I treat others while engaging in the world reflect my faith in ways that are a witness and draw people to Christ. This spills over into how I think about leadership and how I try to lead others when graced with the opportunities to do so.

For any leader, who we model makes a difference in how we lead. If we want to model Jesus, we must *know* him. For Christian leaders, this means negotiating the ways our imperfections can influence others and sidetrack us. We seek to balance our need for perfection with our understanding of a Savior who inundates us with his love, grace, and mercy. We do not get what we deserve. Yet, as disciples of Christ, mirroring him in our leadership as Christians is vital. In fact, our leadership either points people to

Christ or points people away from Christ. If we model a leadership style that is more indicative of the world or corporate America, that is how people will engage with us. This is not to discount what corporate America, or any other model of leadership, has to offer that is consistent with Christian values. However, when behaviors, attitudes, and practices depart from what we say we believe and in whom we say we believe, namely Jesus Christ, then it ought to be a line that we do not cross.

As Christians, we have a goal set before us that prods us to do the work that God has entrusted to us. The ability to do that work as ambassadors for Christ means that we must believe in him and what we are representing about him. What ambassador doesn't believe in the one by whom they've been sent? An effective witness, faithful servant, and authentic Christian leader is also a disciple of Christ. There are many people who can quote Scriptures and who participate in church activities but have never accepted Christ into their heart. Although such a person can be skilled in leading others, something will always be missing in terms of embodying Christ-like leadership if that person isn't a believer.

Christ makes the difference in who we are, how we think, how we treat others, and how we care for ourselves. Because of Christ, our minds and our attitudes are transformed so that we can serve. We have strength to endure and can help others to endure. We can tolerate fickle, erratic, and mean people, and our own attitudes and behaviors will change as we grow and mature. Because of Christ, we can humble ourselves and ask for forgiveness and help when it's necessary. At the very heart of what it means to be a Christian leader is Christ. Christ is the chief cornerstone on which everything else is built.

Christ-like leadership means servant-leadership. While entire books have been written on this topic, it is important to spend some time considering what kind of leader a Christian leader is. I define servant-leadership as primarily focused on and invested in serving and meeting the needs of others. It centers the well-being and growth of others to meet shared goals and objectives and to measure success. Servant-leaders are team-oriented, humble, selfless, and concerned about the common good. Servant-leaders are trustworthy and operate with integrity. While they may have ambition, they do not operate out of selfish ambition. Like Christ, servant-leaders are sacrificial and concerned about the growth and maturity of those they are leading. They are interested in transformation—of people, organizations, communities, and beyond.

In the church as well as in other settings, a servant-leader model has proven to be effective in cultivating authentic and sound Christian leaders. The term "servant-leader" was first coined by Robert Greenleaf in 1970 in an essay entitled, "The Servant as Leader."[1] In the introduction to *The Servant-Leader Within: A Transformative Path*, Larry Spears says this of Greenleaf's model of leadership: "True leadership emerges from those whose primary motivation is a deep desire to help others." This idea encapsulates what it means to be a follower of Christ and to lead as a Christian. The servant-leader model is consistent with what a Christian leader should embody. It identifies how positive change happens, for both the leader and those being led, as well as for the entire community. Indeed, servant-leadership it is what it looks like when 2 Corinthians 5:17 is lived out in the world: to be a new creation in Christ. Greenleaf describes a servant-leader in this way: "The servant-leader is servant first. It begins with the natural feeling that one wants to serve. Then conscious choice brings one to aspire to lead. The best test is: do those served grow as persons; do they, while being served, become healthier, wiser, freer, more autonomous, more likely themselves to become servants?"[2]

This definition highlights the importance of commitment. As Spears indicates, a servant-leader model is not a quick fix but requires time to cultivate a "long-term, transformational approach to life and work—in essence, a way of being—that has the potential for creating a positive change throughout our society."[3] Leadership comes with responsibility. Being a Christian leader means centering the needs and well-being of others in how we lead.

A servant-leader model encapsulates Jesus' heart, mission, and passion and is evident in both his words and his actions. Consider Jesus' instructions to us. In Mark 10:42-45, Jesus calls the disciples together and tells them they're to be countercultural. "You know that among the Gentiles those whom they recognize as their rulers lord it over them, and their great ones are tyrants over them. But it is not so among you; but whoever wishes to become great among you must be your servant, and whoever wishes to be first among you must be slave of all. For the Son of Man came not to be served but to serve, and to give his life a ransom for many." In John 13:13-17, Jesus tells the disciples that he has set the example for them to follow and teach others: "You call me Teacher and Lord—and you are right, for that is what I am. So if I, your Lord and Teacher, have washed your feet, you also ought to wash one another's feet. For I have set you an example, that you also should do as I have done to you. Very truly, I tell you, servants are not greater than their master, nor are messengers greater than the one who sent them. If you know these things, you are blessed if you do them." In Luke 9:23, Jesus alerts the disciples to the sacrificial nature of what it means to be a servant leader: "If any want to become my followers, let them deny themselves and take up their cross daily and follow me."

It's not just what Jesus says—it's in Jesus' actions that we witness servant-leadership. Whether it's washing the disciples' feet, instructing them before sending them out to witness to others, his interaction with the woman at the well and Zacchaeus in a tree, how he engages with the Pharisees and scribes, or hanging between two thieves on a cross, Jesus' interactions with those whom he came to redeem reflect his servant leadership. Indeed, Jesus served humanity and reconciled the world back to God. However, it wasn't just about him, although it is profoundly and absolutely about

Jesus for Christians. It is also about the transformation that happens in the individual's life and the life of the community because of Christ. This is the charge of servant-leaders: to lead in such a way that transformation happens, and we are reconciled and drawn closer to God.

W. Franklyn Richardson amplified the point about servant-leadership being effective leadership in a conversation we had as part of his virtual tour for the release of his book *Witness to Grace: A Testimony of Favor*.[4] Dr. Richardson is the pastor of Grace Baptist Church in Mt. Vernon, New York (my home church) and chair of the Conference of National Black Churches. When I asked him about leading during the pandemic, he highlighted the importance of serving. "If you are driven by the desire to serve people, it will get you to the space you need to be as a leader. The moment it's about you, that moment you lose command to provide leadership. But if you can be driven and undistracted by the need to serve people, to be the people's servant, it will result in effective leadership."[5]

Servant-leadership is also discipleship. Leaders have such a profound effect on people's lives. When Christians lead well, with the well-being of others in mind, discipleship happens in meaningful and life-changing ways. In a Christian context, discipleship is adhering to the instructions, teachings, and examples of Christ. It is how we engage and learn from and with one another in ways that help us to grow and mature in our faith. After accepting Christ into our hearts, we as believers embarks on a journey of faith. However, we are not alone. We are within a community of faith, and many people will sojourn with us throughout our lives at various points along the way.

Discipleship is crucial for Christians (especially Christian leaders) because it helps us to deepen our spiritual well and become spiritually mature. Discipleship helps us to negotiate life's ups and downs and to do the work that God has entrusted to us. It is part of our becoming more like Christ and being equipped for the ministry work God assigns to us. Discipleship determines the tools that equip us for life and living along our journey together as a community of faith. The apostle Paul instructs the church at Ephesus in this way: "Therefore be imitators of God, as beloved children, and live in love, as Christ loved us and gave himself up for us, a fragrant offering and sacrifice to God" (Ephesians 5:1-2).

Without intentional discipleship—putting ourselves in situations where we're discipled and discipling others—we cannot lead effectively. We end up with impotent Christians who have, at best, an elementary understanding of the faith and very little idea of how to walk in the purpose and power God intends. Hebrews 5:12-14 says it this way: "For though by this time you ought to be teachers, you need someone to teach you again the basic elements of the oracles of God. You need milk, not solid food; for everyone who lives on milk, being still an infant, is unskilled in the word of righteousness. But solid food is for the mature, for those whose faculties have been trained by practice to distinguish good from evil." Christian leaders prioritize discipleship. Therefore, they are wise, encouragers, confidantes, teachers, chastisers, standard-keepers, and fruit-bearers. They embody the fruit of the Spirit and strive to reach the high calling that is in Christ Jesus.

An unlikely but intriguing example of discipleship comes from the movie *The Book of Eli* (Alcon Entertainment/Silver Pictures). In the film's post-apocalyptic world, we meet the main character, Eli. He tries to do what God commands of him by delivering the last known copy of the Bible, which is in his possession, to a printing press thousands of miles away. Along the trek, Eli is joined by Solara, who is escaping a villainous businessman that holds her mother hostage. At the same time, the villainous businessman tries to obtain the Bible to be able to "control people's minds." Solara doesn't know much about Eli's mission in the beginning. She is simply escaping a vile and dangerous situation.

Through unbelievable odds and with a lot of violence, Eli and Solara finally reach the printing press in California, which becomes Eli's final resting place. Having given up the book in order to save Solara's life and her mother's, Eli recites the entire content of the Bible to the printer who is then able to make copies. Despite the obstacles and the evil he must fight, Eli remains faithful to his assignment, and his witness rubs off on Solara. While Eli's journey ends, Solara's begins as she puts on his coat, picks up his sword, and sets out to go back to her hometown, presumably to rescue her mother and others along the way. She watched as Eli negotiated the treacherous world left by nuclear catastrophe, with danger lurking around every corner. But rather than stay safely at the compound where the printing press was, she sets out on her own mission, assuming the posture of the one whom she followed, learned from, and eventually emulates. That's an example of discipleship.

We know from Scripture and from history that the disciples discipled others. The spreading of the Good News came through encounters with those ready and willing to give testimony about Christ and to live by his example—to do what Christ did. Discipleship is part of servant-leadership and a vital part of being a Christian leader.

Another important aspect of leading as a Christian has to do with the work of the Holy Spirit in the lives of believers. Embodying the fruit of the Spirit and leading as a Christian is impossible without the Holy Spirit working in and through us. Before ascending to heaven after his resurrection, Jesus let the disciples know that they would not be left alone. Instead, they would receive power when the Holy Spirit came upon them, and they were to wait for this power from on high before doing anything else. As the third person of the Trinity, the Holy Spirit is integral to how Christians are empowered to lead. The Holy Spirit guides, corrects, convicts, settles, grounds, strengthens, and empowers us to do the work God calls us to do. An understanding of how the Holy Spirit works differs within Christian faith traditions. Yet, for those who have the responsibility of leading, being in touch and attuned to the work of the Spirit is key.

Awareness of the Spirit's work happens through prayer, Bible study, practicing the spiritual disciplines, in quiet time with God, and sometimes amid chaos and confusion. It is crucial for Christian leaders to be able to discern when they are being led by the Spirit in their leadership, especially when they are making decisions that will impact others. Being disciples and followers of Christ sometimes means that we will feel led to go in a direction that seems counterintuitive. At times, we may feel as if we're being led to make the hard or unpopular choice. The Holy Spirit fortifies us for the moments when being faithful requires boldness and courage. The Spirit leads and endues us to find the path we will have to take as we lead others. The Spirit sanctifies, molds, and shapes us to grow and mature in our faith and leadership, empowering us to operate fully as ambassadors, as treasures in earthen vessels: "And all of us, with unveiled faces, seeing the glory of the Lord as though reflected in a mirror, are being transformed into the same image from one degree of glory to another; for this comes from the Lord, the Spirit" (2 Corinthians 3:18). Learning to let the Spirit lead us is a spiritual discipline for all Christians, especially Christian leaders.

Christian leadership is also evangelism. Some Christian leaders may feel burdened when thinking about their leadership as evangelism, but there's no way around it. Imagine if every Christian leader related to those they lead and those around them as if they were engaging with Christ. We'd be living in a different world. Yet, when we understand and take seriously our role as ambassadors for Christ, we know that we are the living example of Christ in this world. We are Christ's witnesses.

Many have said, "I'd rather see a sermon than hear one any day." While cliché, it is also true. People do notice how we behave and treat others when we step into leadership roles. The world is filled with those who work with someone or know someone who claims to be Christian, but nothing beyond their words makes it evident that they are. People expect Christian leaders to be different, even when they don't say it.

We who are Christian leaders should also expect something different from ourselves because our standard is neither this world's nor the latest leadership tips from business-school experts nor business magazines. Our standard is Christ. Of course, some people do weaponize someone's bad moment against them or have unrealistic expectations of Christian leaders. However, in our striving to be like Christ—to be Christ-like leaders—we are also showing the world something about the one who we say has sent us, who lives in us, and for whom we've committed our lives. In many ways, how we lead is a living testament to our faith. We witness to Christ by how we treat others and live in the world. This may seem like a high bar for Christian leaders, but I contend that the standard in Christ Jesus *is* high.

Note, contrary to what some would have us to believe, Jesus was not a pushover. Jesus also was not a backstabber, gossiper, deceiver, nor embezzler, nor was he slothful. When we are consistently inconsistent or more concerned about elevating ourselves at the expense of others, we cast a shadow on our faith and open the door for some to question and criticize the one we say we serve. Embodying Christ-like leadership means leaning into the way set before us by the one who is the way, the truth, and the life.

For those leading in secular or interfaith settings, being a Christian leader doesn't mean proselytizing or inappropriately sharing our faith. It means being a sincere, genuine representative of Christ in all the important ways. In other words, even if our behavior in multifaith settings changes, our witness is consistent. We don't have to wear a big cross or another Christian symbol to be a Christian leader. How we behave and treat others matters. It is about our authenticity, not a contrived response or caricature of how a Christian is supposed to behave.

There is another reality. At times, some have led in ways that have been incredibly hurtful and caused church hurt. This can happen even when someone is being careful about the other person's feelings. When we consider the tenets of our faith in our leadership (such as the Golden Rule and the commandment to love one another), we are less likely to hurt people. We bear a responsibility to care about how we lead others, always striving to speak the truth in love, so as to build up and not tear down nor crush someone's spirit.

Moreover, it also important for Christian leaders to understand our relationship with Christ, in addition to how we treat others. In church, we often talk about what it means to have a personal relationship with Christ. The personal impacts the communal, and this is nowhere more evident than it is in Christian leadership. Christ is not a spiritual bellhop who jumps when we ask for things or call out his name in our prayers. Rather, he is the one in whom we have our identity—in whom we live, move, and have our very being. Our belief in Christ ought to be—must be—reflected in how we lead others, no matter the circumstances in which we find ourselves. For effective Christian leaders, Christ is the cornerstone of our leadership as much as he is the chief cornerstone of our faith. This is when our leading becomes servant-leadership and spills over into our discipleship and our evangelism. It is the kind of leadership that we are called to by the one who calls us to serve and to lead others.

Notes

1. Robert K. Greenleaf, *The Servant as Leader* (Cambridge, MA: Center for Applied Studies, 1970).

2. Robert K. Greenleaf, *The Servant-Leader Within: A Transformative Path*, Hamilton Beazley, Julie Beggs, and Larry C. Spears, eds. (Mahwah, NJ: Paulist Press, 2003), 13.

3. Larry C. Spears, "Understanding the Growing Impact of Servant-Leadership," in *The Servant-Leader Within: A Transformative Path*, Hamilton Beazley, Julie Beggs, and Larry C. Spears, eds. (Mahwah, NJ: Paulist Press, 2003), 16.

4. W. Franklyn Richardson, *Witness to Grace: A Testimony of Favor* (Pittsburgh, PA: Church Online, LLC, 2020)

5. To listen to the entire conversation, visit https://www.facebook.com/watch/?v=3933792883310976.

Clarity: Can I Get Some Help, Jesus?

"More important than the quest for certainty is the quest for clarity." —Francois Gautier, journalist

"There's a lot of clarity in hindsight." —Julia Hartz, CEO of Eventbrite

"For we know only in part, and we prophesy only in part; but when the complete comes, the partial will come to an end. When I was a child, I spoke like a child, I thought like a child, I reasoned like a child; when I became an adult, I put an end to childish ways. For now we see in a mirror, dimly, but then we will see face to face. Now I know only in part; then I will know fully, even as I have been fully known."
—1 Corinthians 13:9-12

When I was in divinity school, I took a class on evangelism, ecumenism, and missions. It was one of my favorite classes. The professor, Priscilla Pope-Levison, was also my advisor. She remains a friend, mentor, and confidante. Although our backgrounds are very different, we agreed on a lot of the content in the class, and her passion was contagious.

We read one book that caused me some sleepless nights, and I still wrestle with some of the subject matter. *Silence: A Novel* by Shūsaku Endō is a fictional story about Roman Catholic missionaries in Japan who were forced to apostatize their Christian faith. While they denounced their faith publicly, in some cases, they continued to practice in private. The main character struggled to hear from God, as he was trying to be a missionary in secret in a country where Christians were persecuted. He often felt as if God had abandoned him—and with dire consequences. But in the midst of it all, God was not silent. In one scene, turtle doves were singing as the priest was hoping to hear from God. I interpreted this as God speaking through nature and trying to encourage the priest. Everything in me rejected this notion that God was not present or revealing God's self when the people, particularly these missionaries who were trying to be faithful, most needed to hear from God. The thought of it even now is a challenge for me.[1]

I've been in ministry long enough and have experienced times when the clarity I needed from God did not come. Instead, I had to draw on clarity from a previous moment, a past experience of God that held true for the current circumstance. Most clergy have had moments when they felt that what they needed—God's guidance and clarity—was the very thing they did not have. Don't get me wrong—I still believe and am a witness to the fact that God shows up when needed. However, in seeking to serve God and do God's will, we don't often get step-by-step instructions on how to carry out what we believe God is leading us to do. Sometimes, the best we can do is cry out to God in our prayers, expressing our frustration that God has not responded in a way that confirms it is God prompting us to act. The trumpet does not sound. The angels do not pay a visit to declare "it is so" or "you are blessed and highly favored." In the hardest moments, the situations where there is no easy answer, I have wondered why God wasn't more direct. "Can I get a little help, Jesus?" has been my earnest plea on more than one occasion. I still am not willing to say that God is ever silent, but I certainly understand how someone can think that is the case.

What then are Christian leaders to do with God's apparent silence when dealing with uncertainty? Seeking clarity is a key aspect of leadership in general and Christian leadership in particular. One of the more difficult aspects of the Christian walk is that we rarely, if ever, have detailed instructions for the journey. Ministry, like life, is filled with obstacles, roadblocks, detours, and … the unexpected. The reality is that if we knew all the details ahead of time, we might be more than a little reluctant to move forward! It is, after all, a faith journey. We walk by faith and not by sight. But having *some* sense of clarity, even as we trust God for the uncertain and the unexpected, is necessary for Christian leaders. Without some sense of the direction, purpose, vision, strategic goals, or objectives, we end up going quickly down a road to nowhere. And a road to nowhere is never God's intention unless it is to show us this is where we need to turn around or go in another direction.

Finding clarity is a challenging experience. It is not the same for every situation or circumstance, and each individual finds clarity in different ways. But effective Christian leaders have some understanding of *how* they find clarity as they lead. For that reason, in many ways, clarity is borne out of our experience and relationship with God. I'm not suggesting that someone must have a designated number of years of ministry to have clarity. Rather, as we humbly mature spiritually and go along this journey with God, we also develop spiritual practices and apply spiritual disciplines that help us to discern God's will, direction, and leading.

A pitfall of ministry is that every person and every task can seem important. Often, multiple important things are happening at once. Christian leaders must discern not only what is important but what *their* assignment is in the moment or in dealing with a particular issue—*discernment*. Decisions about what is most important can be hard. However, having clarity about our call and purpose, as well as the mission of the church in the world, helps lead us in the right direction.

Having clarity means having a firm foundation on which to stand. This means that, even when we do not know all the details, we recognize where the boundaries are and the direction in which we are headed. For Christians, some beliefs are non-negotiable: for example, the death, burial, and resurrection of Jesus Christ. If we do not have clarity about this foundation of the Christian faith, then we can be "tossed to and fro and blown about by every wind of doctrine, by people's trickery, by their craftiness in deceitful scheming" (Ephesians 4:14).

Christian leaders must be clear about what it means to be a child of the most high God. Embodying Christ-like leadership means having a solid understanding of and commitment to the Christian faith. In his book *7 Things You Better Have Nailed Down Before All Hell Breaks Loose*, Robert Wolgemuth says, "The best thing that you and I can do is to visit—or revisit—the basics. We need to prepare for all hell breaking loose by building a foundation on which we can safely stand."[2] We can build a foundation by practicing spiritual disciplines such as prayer, fasting, and studying the Scriptures (both Old and New Testaments). It is also important for leaders to recognize that, as Christians, our responsibility and accountability is ultimately to God, not to a denomination, company, organization, or other people. We as pastors, ministers, lay leaders, missionaries, congregants, and Christians serving in other leadership roles are to be an active part of a community of faith—including as a member of a local congregation—where our faith can be strengthened, and we can grow spiritually. Let's look more closely at these disciplines and how they help us to find clarity.

Prayer

The most underutilized and underestimated resource for Christians in general, and for Christian leaders specifically, is prayer. The most basic definition of prayer is communication with God. In prayer, we set aside time to pause to connect with God, recognizing the power, position, authority, and sovereignty of God to not only hear our prayers but also to answer us. Prayer is one of the most powerful tools we have for sound leadership and for our Christian journey.

Yet, too often, Christian leaders neglect to cultivate a meaningful and consistent prayer life. Prayer is essential to our spiritual growth and maturity. Thus, it is essential to Christian leadership. Prayer sustains, fortifies, and encourages us. Prayer helps us to discern how to lead, to develop a vision, and to discern how to best guide the people we are leading. Prayer helps us to stay humble and to keep Christ sovereign over ourselves, our title or position, and other people. Through prayer, we gain wisdom, direction, and peace. Prayer also prepares us to fight the kind of spiritual battles that we will undoubtedly face.

For those in leadership, a consistent time for prayer is key to nurturing a spiritual life and to leading as a Christian. Prayer is a way of life and a posture we should bear through life, constantly seeking, listening, and offering God an open line of communication into our hearts and souls. Too often, we take prayer for granted or offer drive-by prayers where we make requests of God but don't sit quietly or wait for God's response. One of the biggest challenges for Christian leaders is that demands on our time can make it more difficult to sustain a meaningful prayer life. Yet, to maintain clarity, focus, humility, and integrity, prayer must be as integral to the Christian leader's life as breathing. The actual act of praying matters more than the time, place, and format of our prayers. God knows how to meet us where we are, but it helps for us to open the doors (and windows) of communication.

Note, there are probably as many opinions about prayer as there are Christians. The reason we refer to having a *relationship* with God is that the development of our own way of connecting with God is crucial. When I have taught classes on prayer, I provide the formula ACTS. This formula for prayer is based on the Lord's

Prayer: Adoration, Confession, Thanksgiving, and Supplication. While these ingredients can be included in any and all prayers, it is not necessary to always have each one. As Christian leaders, sometimes our prayers will sound more like a lament (Psalm 10:1-2). Other times, they will be a plea to God for direction (Psalm 25:4-5), peace (Numbers 6:24-26), wisdom (James 1:5), or insight (Psalm 119:66). They could also be an urgent request for God to move on our behalf (1 Samuel 1:9-11; Habakkuk 1:2-4).

Sometimes God answers yes, and things move in the direction we want or anticipate. Perhaps more often are the times when the answer is no, or God moves in a different direction from what we want or expect. Sometimes God seems to be silent or tells us to wait for an answer. No right words or formula or ingredients to prayer can "make" God do what we want.

This is why prayer is so essential and why being humble is absolutely necessary. Feeling as if God is not answering our prayers is painful, especially when we believe we are trying to be faithful to the work God has entrusted to us. We may be disappointed when we do our best, and for reasons that we don't understand at that moment, it turns out to be a mess or blows up in our faces. And while a yes to our prayers seems like a good thing, if we are not careful, we might give the impression that *we* are the ones who made something happen rather than that we are experiencing *God's grace*. In fact, it's all grace—the yes to our prayers, the no, the wait, and the silence. The Christian journey, especially that of a Christian leader, is to know that regardless of what's going on, our dependence is on God. While many things are out of our control and beyond our understanding, we are always firmly planted in God's hands.

Humility helps us to be open to God, recognize our faults and shortcomings, and quite frankly, not think more highly of ourselves than we ought. So many Christian leaders miss the importance of humility. Worldly success can make us arrogant if we're not careful.

While nothing is wrong with our being confident in our abilities, being prideful and egotistical makes it hard to have the kind of assurance and clarity that can come only from God. On the other hand, some leaders struggle with their confidence and depend on themselves way too much as they try to negotiate feelings of inadequacy and the *imposter syndrome*.[3] In either case, having humility allows us to balance our inadequacies with God's sufficiency and our arrogance with God's omnipotence.

The reality is that not having our prayers answered the way we want or expect can be extremely disheartening. No one wants to put forth their best efforts only to have them fail. However, when we are put in roles of leadership, sometimes our best efforts do not turn out the way we want them to. While prayer doesn't always get us what we want, it does connect us to the Source, the Creator and Sustainer, the Way Maker and Provider—and we are never forsaken. This is my witness and my testimony. When one of my favorite uncles died, a close friend of mine said to me, "We submit to God's will." It was painful, but it also resonated with me. I had prayed for a different outcome. I *believed* in God for a different outcome. But in the end, I submitted to God's will. In so many ways, prayer is a recognition, an acknowledgment that in our lives, we are submitting to God's will and not our own. As the Lord's Prayer says, "Thy will be done on earth as it is in heaven."

Prayer is a way of being, a posture that we have as we lead others and as we're being led. As Christian leaders, we should discipline ourselves to develop a lifestyle of prayer. Before we make a move, minute or substantial, we should pause and take a moment to pray. Barbara Williams-Skinner, a mentor and friend who leads the Skinner Leadership Institute, and I have talked about this at length. We have wondered out loud if Christian leaders spend enough time in prayer. On the surface, it seems that many do not. I cannot say that I always have. We have imagined together what the world would be like, how our government would work, how communities would thrive, how so many of the social ills that plague us might be different if prayer was as much a part of us as breathing. Prayer is not a magic wand. But what I do know is that when we incorporate prayer into our daily routines and take a few moments to center ourselves in God and to ask God for guidance and direction (even in the small things), we experience a big difference in our outlook, in how we lead, and in the decisions we make.

Christian leaders have the privilege and responsibility to not only pray for themselves but also to consistently pray for those whom they are leading. In praying, it is important to be mindful to pray *for* people not just about them. Although our inclination may be to pray that those we are leading behave and act the way we want (praying *about* them), it is crucial that Christian leaders also pray for their well-being and spiritual growth, and that their relationship with God is strengthened, among other requests that have nothing to do with our leading them (praying *for* them). Any leader can testify that leading people can be taxing. People can be difficult, mean, unruly, rude, stubborn, exhausting, and can try our patience. But ultimately, Christian leadership, regardless of the setting, is not just about us and what we want or need. It is just as much about the people whom we are leading—how we are equipping them, and journeying with them, to live into their God-given purpose. Only praying to God about them and not actually praying *for* them does not help us to lead any better. In many ways, it is a two-pronged effort.

Some may ask what the point of prayer is if the desired outcome is not granted. Prayer is not about the outcome but rather about having an open heart, mind, and spirit. It's about trusting God for our daily circumstances and the direction of our lives. It's about receiving the peace that passes all understanding and recognizing that some things are outside of our control.

During the coronavirus pandemic, we had so much to pray for and lift before God. We were navigating uncharted territory, living in fear of a virus that at one point took the lives of more than three thousand people a day. Many Christian leaders faced a plethora of issues converging in what felt like total chaos—concentrated grief, an economic crisis, racial disparities, social upheaval, overall health concerns, and a complete overhaul of all that had been familiar. The whole world was turned upside down. Pastors and lay leaders moved worship services online and found creative ways to do ministry. Our normal religious practices—funeral services, baby dedications or baptisms, corporate worship, fellowship, Bible study, prayer meeting, and Sunday school—were either put on hold, canceled, or reconfigured as virtual experiences.

With so much uncertainty, many experienced what Dexter Nutall, pastor of New Bethel Baptist Church in Washington, DC, called "prayer fatigue." This feeling certainly isn't confined to the pandemic. There are seasons in the life of a Christian leader when it can feel as if we are going to God with such heavy burdens that it is mentally and physically exhausting to pray. In these moments when we have little control and lots of concerns, when we need assurances but only have questions, God meets us in our prayer time. This is when our faith is tested and tried in a refiner's fire. Romans 8:26 says, "Likewise the Spirit helps us in our weakness; for we do not know how to pray as we ought, but that very Spirit intercedes [for us] with sighs too deep for words." When we are weary and tired, when we need encouragement and strength, prayer helps to fortify and settle us and gives us enough clarity for today and maybe tomorrow as well.

Prayer equips Christian leaders to deal with spiritual warfare. It's helpful to think of spiritual warfare as obstacles, battles, temptations, or roadblocks we face in trying to accomplish the goals and tasks before us. It can take us by surprise or throw us off our game if we are not ready for it or don't recognize it. Not every obstacle or difficulty is necessarily spiritual warfare, but there are times when the challenge, struggle, or situation is quite intense and unusually difficult. At those times, it is important to recognize that we are not just fighting what we see and experience in the natural. It is also a spiritual battle.

Ephesians 6:10-16 is a key Scripture passage that brings this struggle to light. In this passage, the apostle Paul explains that we wrestle not against flesh and blood, but "against the rulers, against the authorities, against the cosmic powers of this present darkness, against the spiritual forces of evil in the heavenly places." Paul's words remind us to equip ourselves with the "full armor" of God—the belt of truth, the breastplate of righteousness, feet shod with the gospel of peace, the shield of faith, the helmet of salvation, and the sword of the Spirit. Therefore, we are to "pray in the Spirit." Doing so will help us to stand firm and to have clarity when what we're facing is beyond our natural abilities to handle. It is impossible to know fully what we may be fighting against when we are dealing with spiritual warfare, but prayer helps us to activate our faith and be properly prepared "to stand against the wiles of the devil."

We Christians can live with the assurance that God is with us and will never leave us or forsake us. We are further promised that Jesus sits at the right hand of God making intercessions for us. Even the impossible is possible with God, and God sometimes grants us our requests to heal, deliver, move on our behalf, provide for us, and make a way when there seems to be no way. Sometimes God seems to move too slowly or refuses to move at all, at least from the perspective of the one praying. Further, sometimes the miracle we are looking for doesn't happen, while occasionally the miraculous emerges with brilliance and splendor. I wish I had a guidebook on which prayers would be answered and which ones would not. But even when we do not get the answers we want, God is still listening to and answering our prayers. And even when we are experiencing a deafening silence from God despite our urgent need to hear *something*, it doesn't mean that God is not working on our behalf.

Fasting

I was once asked to teach a class on fasting. At the time, it seemed like a strange ask of me. Then, I realized that the discipline of fasting is one that has become a part of my spiritual practices, especially when I need to connect with God on a deeper level than what my daily routine allows. The Gospel of Mark records an encounter with Jesus and the disciples after the disciples had been unable to heal a boy. When he had entered the house, his disciples asked him privately, "Why could we not cast it out?" He said to them, "This kind can come out only through prayer and fasting" (Mark 9:28-29, NRSVUE) Fasting can open our spirit to hear from God in a way that we would otherwise not be able to do.

Fasting can be done in different ways. Essentially, fasting is to abstain from eating in order to spend that time in prayer or another spiritual practice. When fasting, we focus our attention on God and how God might be leading us. Rather than fasting from food, some people will give up other activities that are important to them to concentrate on their relationship with God. This might include giving up television, social media, computer games, or other activities to focus on prayer. Prayer and fasting go hand in hand. And it is often said that fasting without prayer is just going on a diet rather than exercising a spiritual discipline.

Fasting can be beneficial for Christian leaders in so many ways. It can open us to new possibilities and help us to grow spiritually. It can give us vision, wisdom, and insight about a situation, decision, or opportunity we are thinking about pursuing. Fasting can help us let go of burdens we've been carrying, allowing us to consider all the different options. It is sacrificial and prompts us not to concentrate on ourselves, our problems, or our circumstances, but instead to focus solely on God and God's will for our lives. Fasting and prayer coupled with times of solitude and meditation are proven ways to get clarity from God on direction, decisions, a plan of action, determining goals, or other ways that God might be moving or leading us to go.

Fasting can also help us to identify why we may be frustrated in our prayer life or feel as if our prayers are going no further than the ceiling. When we feel we are experiencing impediments to our prayers, fasting can move us to a healthier spiritual place. Unforgiveness, bitterness, disappointment, and unresolved anger are all barriers that can make us feel as if our prayers are stunted. Fasting can help us to both identify the barriers in our lives and resolve or move toward resolving them.

Studying Scriptures

For Christian leaders, studying our sacred texts is paramount for finding clarity when we seek it. While numerous contemporary debates about interpretation and the inerrancy of the Bible exist, it is no understatement to say that Christian leaders should have some knowledge of Scripture. I come from a Baptist faith tradition in which memorizing and knowing the Bible are central.

Regardless of tradition, Christians should be familiar with the sacred texts and traditions of our faith. Christian leaders bear a responsibility to spend time studying God's Word. When we study Scripture, it encourages us, informs us of God's promises, reminds us of who we are as God's children, instructs us on God's ways, and teaches us about God's character. In the moments when human reasoning doesn't make any sense, Scripture can provide us with insight and direction, a kind of clarity that we cannot obtain elsewhere. Scripture undergirds our prayers and models how and what to pray. Having a foundational and healthy understanding of the Bible goes a long way in maintaining a sense of clarity in our own lives as we seek to lead others. Psalm 119:105 says it beautifully; "Your word is a lamp to my feet and a light to my path."

Scripture helps us to understand God's character. This is relevant because, in times when we are wondering about how God is moving in our lives or what God may (or may not) be calling us to do or to endure, Scripture offers guiding knowledge and understanding of God's character. If we understand that God is a Provider, then even when we are experiencing a lack like the Shunammite woman (2 Kings 4:8-37), we can lean on God's promise to provide. When we know that God loves us with an *agape*—unconditional—kind of love, we can trust that God will never leave us nor forsake us. Once we've experienced God breaking down barriers and working on our behalf, we are more confident that God is a way maker. When we recognize that God can turn even dire situations around, like Jesus did for the woman with an issue of blood and Jairus' daughter (Mark 5:21-43), then we can also believe that God is able to do the same for us. Isaiah 55:11 puts it this way: "So shall my word be that goes out from my mouth; it shall not return to me empty, but it shall accomplish that which I purpose, and succeed in the thing for which I sent it." Studying and knowing Scripture is essential for our leadership as well as our personal lives.

Church Membership

People have many reasons not to go to church or become a part of a local congregation. Churches can be a mess. People can try your patience. Gossip can sometimes fill the sanctuary just as easily as praise. Some people are mean and unwelcoming. Others seem to be distant, aloof, and judgmental. Sadly, those who should be the most trustworthy and the easiest to work with are too often unreliable and hostile. And the hypocrites! My goodness—there seem to be a lot of them.

In some ways, these are stereotypes about churches; sometimes, the description fits the bill all too well. Yet, this description does not tell the whole story about church and what it means to be a part of a local congregation. Churches are places where lifelong friendships are made, souls are nurtured, children are cared for, and families are supported. There is nothing like gathering in person for worship or prayer services and joining our voices, hearts, and minds with other people of faith. Certainly, the pandemic has demonstrated how important weekly services are in our lives. While sexual abuse, financial impropriety, and other shortcomings—all of which are inexcusable—exist, there are many healthy congregations where people can grow, thrive, and develop their spiritual gifts and skills. They are also places where clarity can happen.

Living life within a community of believers who regularly share their faith journey with one another helps us to develop and grow, as well as to have a sense of responsibility and accountability. As we participate in corporate worship, rituals, small groups, and Bible studies, as we listen to the testimonies of others and share our own, we gain a sense of God and how God works and shows up in the lives of God's people. We also develop *spiritual eyes and ears* that help us to discern what's going on around us, and we learn how to respond and govern ourselves accordingly. Being a part of a local congregation helps us to learn so much about ourselves and how we can and should lead others. These leadership building blocks cannot be replaced by being a part of a virtual church outside of one's own community. It doesn't mean that we should not regularly listen to a favorite pastor or choir online. Christian leaders also must be connected to a local congregation where they can serve, mature, and connect in a more intimate way to the body of Christ.

Having clarity is an important and significant part of Christian leadership. It is not the same thing as having certainty, but it is crucial to be able to lead others. While there are no step-by-step instructions about how to get absolute clarity, we can employ spiritual disciplines and practices to be as clear about our purpose, direction, and vision as possible. In other words, by living out our Christian faith with intentionality, we can gain clarity for our spiritual journey and for leading others.

For example, my daughter and my son used to be avid soccer players. They played from the time they were young and still loved the sport. As they grew up, they learned the fundamentals of the sport: the language, the positions, the rules of the game. They know who was supposed to be doing what and when they were supposed to be doing it. They not only played on teams but also attended camps and skill-building clinics to improve upon the fundamental skills that they learned. They watched soccer games on television. They watched others play the game. They watched the best of the best execute the drills—the same drills that they practiced with precision and excellence so that they could be better as well.

In the same way, being part of a community of faith helps us to learn the language of faith. It helps us to build upon our fundamental understanding and begin to learn from others who are practicing the faith. Leading without clarity is like trying to win a game without a game plan. Christian leaders must have clarity about those things that will not change—the fundamentals of the faith, their call, and the direction, purpose, and mission of the church. Just as each soccer player knows their position on the field, a Christian leader's call will help to determine what their assignment is. In addition, knowing Scripture provides the foundation and game plan for the way forward. Practicing the faith and exercising the fundamentals will allow us to walk in purpose and fulfill the mission of the congregation both locally and worldwide. It also helps us to be ambassadors for Christ and witnesses as we lead others outside of the church. Without clarity, we are more easily swayed and distracted by things that have no relevance or significance for the work that God has placed into our hands. It is also so much harder to embody Christian leadership if we do not have clarity. On the other hand, when we have clarity, we are able to fulfill the assignments that God has entrusted to us.

Notes
1. Shūsaku Endō, translated by William Johnston, *Silence: A Novel* (New York: Picador Modern Classics, 2016).
2. Robert Wolgemuth, 7 *Things You Better Have Nailed Down Before All Hell Breaks Loose* (Nashville: Thomas Nelson, 2008), xiv.
3. Gill Corkindale, "Overcoming Imposter Syndrome," Harvard Business Review (2008), accessed April 25, 2022.

Character: No Jokers Allowed

"You can't buy character."—Bishop Donald Hilliard, senior pastor of Cathedral International in Perth Amboy, New Jersey[1]

"And not only that, but we also boast in our sufferings, knowing that suffering produces endurance, and endurance produces character, and character produces hope, and hope does not disappoint us, because God's love has been poured into our hearts through the Holy Spirit that has been given to us." —Romans 5:3-5

A historic church in a large urban area was seeking a new pastor to lead their congregation. One candidate was particularly charismatic and seemed to be exactly what they were looking for. He showed up with his wife for one of the interviews. By all appearances, he had a model family and ministry. But some members searched the Internet and found out that he was not quite who he presented himself to be. However, the church decided to offer him the job to lead the congregation anyway. Months after his installation, he had divorced and remarried, showing up to church with a different wife than the one who was there with him in the interview. A year or so later, he was facing criminal charges for assault. Several years later, he was still the pastor while church membership had dwindled, and the church was in turmoil.

The church and the world are desperate for Christian leaders who have good character. With so many world leaders falling because of scandal, even those outside the church long for Christian leaders to be different. It is not enough for someone to be gifted or to express with great clarity and authenticity the mysteries of the faith. It is not sufficient for someone to be dynamic or charismatic. There is absolutely nothing wrong with being gifted or dynamic or charismatic, but those qualities are not the same thing as being a person with character and integrity. Gifts are not fruit, and charisma is not character.

The apostle Paul says, "The gifts and the calling of God are irrevocable" (Romans 11:29). Someone can use their gifts to be a tremendous blessing to the body of Christ, but that does not mean that the person is spiritually mature or exhibiting the fruit of the Spirit: love, joy, peace, patience, kindness, generosity, faithfulness, gentleness, and self-control (Galatians 5:22-25). Being gifted does not preclude us from falling into sinful behaviors and attitudes, nor does it prohibit us from being mean and nasty individuals. Spiritual maturity, the work of the Spirit, and personal growth work together to transform us into leaders with good moral character. A changed heart and transformed mind drive good character and make effective Christian leaders.

Therefore, the transformative work of the Holy Spirit is a crucial part of the Christian leader's life. Indeed, we expect that someone who is a Christian leader is also someone who has been transformed by the Holy Spirit. We hope that someone who is a Christian leader exhibits the fruit of the Spirit. Sadly, that is not always the case. Too often, what happens in our churches (and in secular contexts) is that we mistake a person's gifts for their character. We assume that, because someone can preach great sermons or pray impressive prayers, this person walks with integrity. More often than we'd like to admit, we are wrong about this assumption.

Consequently, disingenuous and duplicitous charlatans who seek to take advantage of God's people or who have no intentions of living by God's precepts are given positions of authority in the church, faith-based groups, or other organizations. I'm not referring to someone having a bad day, which can happen to even the most committed Christian leader. I'm talking about deliberate, intentional, and consistent behavior that is immoral, chaotic, or dishonest— behavior that causes harm and confusion and is done for selfish gain. These are people whom I often refer to as *jokers*. Jokers are the church leaders who steal the money, not by accident of accounting, but by a scheme that they devised. These are the church leaders who run through the church, engaging in inappropriate relationships with numerous parishioners, wreakinig havoc and divisions. In other settings, jokers might be the ones who purport their Christian faith, but their actions do not align with Christian values and often shine a negative light on the Christian faith. Jokers are the ones who end up on the news with some version of the headline, "Church leader arrested for...." I don't intend to be disparaging by casting these people in a negative light. Yet, there are those who deliberately take advantage of God's people and exhibit no integrity in how they govern themselves or handle God's business.

Admittedly, it is hard to talk about character without fear of seeming preachy or judgmental. Our faith tells us that none of us is perfect, and anyone can be used by God—even a donkey. Ask Balaam (Numbers 22:21-39). However, our faith also lifts up a standard by which we should live and strive to be our best selves. Paul says it this way: "So if anyone is in Christ, there is a new creation: everything old has passed away; see, everything has become new!" (2 Corinthians 5:17). We may not be completely different people, but there should be a difference in Christian leaders that demonstrates that they have been made new. Minimally, we should strive to have good character as Christian leaders, because our behavior doesn't just reflect us—it also reflects God.

It is essential for Christian leaders to have good character that witnesses to the salvific and transforming power of the one whom we follow and proclaim died that we might have life and have it more abundantly. Again, I'm not talking about perfection but character. In his book *The Making of a Preacher*, McMickle makes a similar point—that God can use anyone: "God reserves the right to call into ministry anyone God chooses, including persons whose sinful past might have disqualified them in the eyes of everyone but God."[2] My focus on character as it pertains to Christian leaders in some ways agrees with McMickle's claim that God can use anyone. I know this to be true. Yet, irrespective of what someone used to do or who they once were, those who occupy space, authority, and positions as Christian leaders must attend to the issues of their character. For those operating in Christian leadership roles, character counts.

Character matters the most when things do not go as planned or when one is faced with difficult decisions. It makes a difference in how we view and operate in the world. It governs how we treat people—especially people whom we do not see as being on our level or on our side. Character makes a difference in how we *lead*. It is especially important when no one is watching, when you could potentially do something immoral or unethical. Character counts. And people watch to see what Christian leaders do and how they respond when faced with moral dilemmas. They observe how we engage with the world, what our priorities are, and how we uphold our Christian values as they intersect or interact with secular ones. What the world has seen hasn't always been exemplary and, in some instances, has been downright despicable. For example, consider the Christian leader who is convicted of embezzling money but refuses to apologize or resign; the leader who gets caught in a compromising sexual situation and then changes their teachings on sex outside of marriage to excuse their behavior; or the one who is a part of a hate group but says they love and respect the people of color who are a part of their congregation.

Take also the example of the pandemic. Public health officials recommended wearing masks to slow the spread of the novel coronavirus. Many municipalities began to mandate them in public places, as did the federal government. In the early days of the pandemic, the social distancing and sanitation guidelines rendered the normal practices of church risky. These guidelines meant that funeral services, baby dedications and baptisms, Communion, and other rituals of the church stopped, went online, or were adjusted to accommodate COVID-19 protocols. It was a lot to ask, but lives were literally at risk. Early on, it became obvious that the coronavirus was not like the flu or a cold, as many people lost their lives within weeks of contracting the virus. Hospitals were overrun, and the healthcare system was on the verge of collapse.

The pandemic both revealed and aggravated social tensions and disparities, as the elderly, those with compromised immune systems, and people from Black, Brown, and Indigenous communities were particularly vulnerable to getting seriously ill and dying. Asian Americans and Pacific Islanders faced harassment and discrimination because the virus was thought to have originated in an Asian country. The world was in chaos. If ever there was a time that leadership was needed, especially sound Christian leaders, it was then—and now.

Yet, some Christian leaders adamantly advocated for people to continue doing business as usual.[3] They persisted with in-person, unmasked worship services. They couched it as a matter of faith, some likening wearing a mask to not having faith in God. Others employed erroneous theology, saying God would protect them from the virus. Some Christian leaders suggested that the elderly should sacrifice their lives for the economy to open back up! One particularly prominent leader said the elderly have had a good life and should be willing to sacrifice it for the economy and their grandchildren. Where is that in the Bible?[4]

Once a vaccine became available, some of the same pastoral leaders, elected officials, and media personalities who claimed to be Christians discouraged people from getting vaccinated. By the end of 2020, nearly 350,000 people had died in the US alone from COVID-19. By the end of 2021, more than 800,000 people had died. In the first half of 2022, the US crossed the dismal milestone of more than 1 million deaths from the novel coronavirus. Suggesting that people shouldn't get vaccinated or take simple measures to ensure they and others were protected was not only irresponsible, reckless leadership, it was a moral failure. It was also deadly.

Ironically, many who claimed to be pro-life refused to wear masks, even when it was proven to be an effective method of slowing the spread of the coronavirus and saving lives. Some Christian leaders offered messages around personal freedom, and some went as far as to say the vaccine was the "mark of the beast" referenced in Revelation 13.[5] While people had different reasons for not being vaccinated—not just bad theology—consistently wearing a mask to help save lives should not have been controversial. Staying home to protect the elderly or others who were vulnerable should not have been debatable. These actions reflected poorly on the Christian faith as a whole, not just those individuals. It will take a long time to undo the damage done by these leaders. And the work to rebuild trust falls on *all* Christian leaders, not just those who misled people.

Note, if your personal theology always lines up with what will benefit you, make you comfortable, or make you financially more secure, then it may be appropriate to engage in a comprehensive spiritual check and consider your theological perspective. When Christian leaders base their identity and their theology on Christ, we bear a sacrificial nature in who we are, what we do, and how we lead. At some point, we need to take up the cross and deny ourselves. Our ministry and our work are *not* about us.

Poor character coupled with possession of authority equals a mess. In fact, many church messes we witness are the result of this toxic combination. For this reason, it is vitally important for churches to be both discerning and meticulous about those whom they ask to be in leadership positions. Churches should not only simply be persuaded by the gifts that they see, but also seek evidence of the fruit of the Spirit and spiritual maturity. In addition, due diligence requires more than conducting a credit report or checking a candidate's references. True diligence means conducting a criminal background check (especially for those working with children and vulnerable populations) and obtaining psychological examinations as well. For churches that do not have psychological assessments as part of their ordination process, contracting with a licensed Christian counselor or another practitioner to administer an exam and provide an evaluation would be beneficial. Checking the candidate's presence on social media and contacting people not on their list of references are also important. Platforms like LinkedIn can show mutual connections, and touching base with denominational offices or local ministerial alliances are other ways of doing due diligence.

The importance of the steps outlined above is beyond mere procedure. To understand how the Holy Spirit is operating in their lives, we must take the time to look beneath the surface and discern whether the person is someone who has character and integrity and is open to the transformative power of the Holy Spirit. As Christians, all of us are sinners saved by grace. And, yes, we struggle sometimes to do what we know is right. However, there should be some evidence somewhere that our lives are changed *and changing*. It's important for churches to make sure the street hustler or corporate executive who begins attending the local congregation and seeks leadership positions is more than looking for a way to move their game from the streets or boardroom into the church, for example.

I'm reminded of the character Elmer Gantry from the novel of the same title by Sinclair Lewis. In the book, Gantry was a con artist and hustler who figured out that he could make lots of money by swindling church people. He was a charismatic tent-revival type of preacher, and people soaked in everything he said. His preaching often made no sense at all, especially not from a theological perspective. It was all flash and no substance. Yet, people continuously elevated him and welcomed him, which gave him opportunities to deceive and scam God's people. His success only increased as he aligned himself with a woman evangelist who was also very charismatic.

Elmer Gantry's gifts were not indicative of his being a new creation in Christ. He was not "growing in grace," as he did many of the things he preached against. The problem was not that he had faults. The problem was that he really had no issue with his shortcomings—he worked on becoming a better scam artist! He didn't struggle with his ethical dilemma—he simply tried to get rich from people who believed he was forthright. Most significantly, Gantry was not a believer. He pretended to be one for his own profit.

There is a distinction between an Elmer Gantry-type and a Christian leader who has a fall from grace or who makes an error in judgment that profoundly impacts the people they lead. Some Christian leaders have good character and intentions but mess up in ways that jeopardize their ministries and have people question their motivations. Any leader is susceptible to this happening to them. When someone grows prideful or is burned out and in need of a break, they are more likely to experience lapses in judgment or make mistakes.

To be clear, it is not immoral to make a mistake. Christian leaders with good character make mistakes all the time. That is why it is important to stay humble and to admit to and fix errors that we make. It's critical for Christian leaders who make mistakes to repent and apologize for their actions. Christian leaders are susceptible to pride, ego, arrogance, greed, envy, and other vices. Christian leaders have character flaws like everyone else. That is why personal growth, spiritual maturity, and the transformative work of the Holy Spirit are important.

Elmer Gantry was published in 1927, and as Solomon said in Ecclesiastes 1:9 (NIV), "What has been will be again, what has been done will be done again; there is nothing new under the sun." News reports and anecdotal evidence suggest that the type of pastor that Lewis caricatures in Elmer Gantry is still present in the church today. While there is nothing new, certain nuances about contemporary society amplify the significance of having good character. Technological advances, as well as a toxic and divisive political climate that spills over into the church, underscore the role that character plays in the Christian leader's life. Christian leaders should be above the fray and operate with integrity. In fact, we should embody integrity and consistently be aware of and grapple with the areas of our lives that need work and growth. It's not enough for Christian leaders to say, "I'm not perfect" without also saying "I'm working on it"—and having evidence to show that is the case.

Many people who are gifted and have potential are new to the faith. I am not suggesting that people who are in this category should be excluded from serving in leadership roles. I am saying, however, that being gifted is not a stand-alone criterion for Christian leadership. Gifts must be coupled with character and spiritual maturity. To develop good leaders, churches must take mentoring relationships seriously and create opportunities for growth. All Christian leaders should have accountability partners and mentors who care about them. People in these roles should want the best for them—not just success defined by worldly criteria, but faithfulness according to God's standards.

Accountability partners and mentors are not the same thing, although sometimes these roles overlap. Accountability partners are those people who journey with us in life and living. They care about us being our best selves and fulfilling our God-given purpose. Accountability partners are people who will tell us the truth and who will offer a word of rebuke or correction if needed. They are not people who want something from us or think we can open doors for them. Conversely, they are not people from whom we want something, or who we think might open doors for us. Accountability partners are people with whom we are in mutual relationship and in whom we trust to have our best interests at heart. They are people we will listen to when we are about to make a mistake or go down a road that should be avoided.

Accountability partners are important when faced with a challenge or a temptation to do something that is not reflective of our character or beliefs. In other words, they are people who can help us make wise decisions and offer a word of correction if we've made a foolish one. We all need accountability partners to confer with and to give us a spiritual check on our words, thoughts, emotions, and actions. Someone whom you don't respect or whose advice you won't heed cannot be an accountability partner for you.

Similarly, a mentor is someone you admire, who has blazed a path you want to follow or is doing the work you are doing or hope to do. They do not necessarily have to be in the same field but can be modeling the type of work ethic and witness to the world that you feel called to emulate. In many ways, mentors are lifting as they climb, while accountability partners are, for the most part, on the same rung of the ladder with you. The bottom line is that Christian leaders should have others traveling with them on the Christian journey—sojourners—at multiple junctures and through various seasons of life.

Regardless of whether someone is a new leader or a seasoned one, all spiritual leaders need a plan for their growth and development—something that goes far beyond simple training in how to preach a good sermon, run meetings, and greet first-time visitors. An intentional spiritual plan for developing Christian leaders is essential, so leaders can fully operate in their gifts while they develop new skills to lead others, grow spiritually, and become more firmly grounded in their faith.

McMickle raises another important point about character. He asks whether preachers should be models or mirrors of character for others. He cautions that "none of us is qualified to be a model for how others should live their lives. We are too prone to get caught up in the sins of the flesh set forth in Galatians 5:19-21, which include jealousy, selfishness, fits of rage, sexual immorality, hatred, discord, and envy."[6]

Instead, McMickle lifts up Jesus as the only "consistent and unfailing model for the behavior of others." While this is true, Christians have different understandings of how Jesus modeled leadership. Thankfully, no leadership model is one-size-fits-all, not even when we are all following Jesus. Part of God's creative genius is that we are individually wrapped with our own gifts, talents, skills, and graces, which may be similar, but are never exactly the same. McMickle describes the difference between a model and a mirror as follows: "If models say this person's example reflects how we should live, a mirror is a person whose life reflects the struggles and shortfalls that we are actually living." He continues to say that rather than model, every preacher knows there have been times when "our lives perfectly mirrored the same struggles we see going on in the lives of those to whom we preach."[7]

Certainly, some of the most effective Christian leaders are those who can be transparent enough to be mirrors instead of models.

It's not necessary to craft a perfect persona. After all, nobody can really live up to perfection. Seeing people lead with and through their imperfections demonstrates how we depend on God, and not solely on ourselves. As mirrors, we can give an authentic glimpse of the ups and downs experienced by Christian leaders as they seek to live out their call and purpose in the world. This idea is perfectly illustrated in 2 Corinthians 12:9-10, where the apostle Paul tells the church at Corinth about the *thorn in his flesh*: "But he said to me, 'My grace is sufficient for you, for my power is made perfect in weakness.' So, I will boast all the more gladly about my weaknesses, so that Christ's power may dwell in me. Therefore I am content with weaknesses, insults, hardships, persecutions, and calamities for the sake of Christ; for whenever I am weak, then I am strong (NIV)."

Finally, a word about conflict. Far too many Christian leaders try to avoid all conflict. In a conversation with Traci Blackmon, a pastor, denominational leader, and friend of mine, she rightly points out that there are people who confuse being conflict-adverse with being conflict-setting. Just because you call out an issue doesn't mean you caused it to happen. Additionally, not calling something out that is wrong doesn't make it go away. Silence is not the same as peace. This is critically important to understand since "iron sharpens iron" (Proverbs 27:17), and we will be made better people and leaders by investing in each other's spiritual and personal growth and maturity.

We want to be the best that we can be and to constantly be growing, maturing, and gaining wisdom. That cannot happen if no one cares enough to check us on our behavior or our way of thinking. Caring sometimes means risking telling us about something important, even when doing so may cause conflict between us. Christian leaders can have differences of opinion without hating each other, even if it results in conflict. But I cannot tell you how many Christian leaders I've met who *cause* exponentially more conflict by trying to avoid it. Avoiding conflict is exhausting and counter-productive. Rather than ignore or gloss over issues, it is beneficial to all involved to find the words and space to offer correction in love or to express a difference of opinion. I suggest that love *requires* that we address conflict rather than ignore it. Christian leaders must be conflict resolvers so that we nurture honest and authentic relationships and maintain a clear conscience in how we deal with people.

Managing conflict is also a gossip stopper. Addressing issues or a conflict directly with those involved helps everyone to be in right relationship. It prevents detrimental and unhealthy side conversations, which don't resolve conflict, solve problems, build relationships, or move us toward achieving our goals. In her book *Dare to Lead*, Brené Brown points to a slogan attributed to an Alcoholics Anonymous meeting: "Clear is kind. Unclear is unkind."[8] Sometimes having the hard conversations shows more character than being silent and saying nothing.

It is also important to say a word about abusive people who are Christians and in leadership positions. Like it or not, there are abusers in our midst. These abusive personalities include those who are verbally, emotionally, physically, or spiritually abusive. Sometimes, abusive people can appear very charismatic, nice, and friendly. Some may even seem "harmless." But they can cause considerable harm and, while restoration is possible, Christian leaders should have a no-tolerance policy for abuse.

The challenge, of course, is identifying abusive people in the church. I'm often struck by how many people comment on how the sexual abuser or child predator "seemed so nice" or that they "would have never guessed that the person was an abuser." If we could tell who they are, we would never let them get into the positions where they could abuse people and cause so much harm. In other words, abusers don't look like what we think abusers look like, in most cases. However, once we recognize abusive behavior and tendencies, it is critically important for us to call the person into accountability. They may need counseling or another kind of additional support. They likely should step aside from their leadership position until the issues are resolved. Ignoring abusive behaviors and/or blaming the victim for that behavior are not appropriate responses. It is also critical not to turn away nor to bury our heads in the sand, pretending that the abuse is not happening or that it will go away without being addressed because we are benefitting from the gifts of the abuser.

Character is important for Christian leaders and is essential for embodying Christ-like leadership. While the tale of unethical Christian leader who steals the money or sexually abuses a child seems like an old story, it is one that gets replayed repeatedly with different names, places, churches, and faith-based organizations. No matter where it happens, it has the same devastating impact on the individuals and congregations involved as well as the broader community. We all must take seriously the *community* aspect of faith community. This means ensuring, to the best of our ability, that Christian leaders build their character as they also build their knowledge of God and build up the people they serve.

Notes

1. Donald Hilliard (@Bishop_Hilliard), "You can't buy character," Twitter, February 4, 2022.

2. Marvin A. McMickle, *The Making of a Preacher: 5 Essentials for Ministers Today* (Valley Forge, PA: Judson Press, 2018), 57.

3. Jaclyn Cosgrove, "L.A. megachurch pastor mocks pandemic health orders, even as church members fall ill," *Los Angeles Times* (El Segundo, CA), November 8, 2020, https://www.latimes.com/california/story/2020-11-08/la-pastor-mocks-covid-19-rules-church-members-ill.

4. Alex Samuels, "Dan Patrick says 'there are more important things than living and that's saving this country,'" *The Texas Tribune* (Austin, TX), April 21, 2020, https://www.texastribune.org/2020/04/21/texas-dan-patrick-economy-coronavirus/.

5. Elizabeth Dwoskin, "On social media, vaccine misinformation mixes with extreme faith," *The Washington Post* (Washington, DC), February 16, 2021,

https://www.washingtonpost.com/technology/2021/02/16/covid-vaccine-misinformation-evangelical-mark-beast/.

Scott Gleeson and Asha Gilbert, "Some say COVID-19 vaccine is the 'mark of the beast.' Is there a connection to the Bible?," *USA Today*, September 26, 2021, https://www.usatoday.com/story/news/nation/2021/09/26/covid-vaccine-mark-beast-what-book-revelation-says/8255268002/.

6. McMickle, *The Making of a Preacher*, 60.

7. McMickle, 60–61.

8. Brené Brown, *Dare to Lead: Brave Work. Tough Conversations. Whole Hearts.* (New York: Random House Publishing Group, 2018), 44.

Courage: Paging Queen Vashti

"Courage is the most important of all the virtues, because without courage you can't practice any other virtue consistently. You can practice any virtue erratically, but nothing consistently without courage."
—Maya Angelou[1]

"I hereby command you: Be strong and courageous; do not be frightened or dismayed, for the LORD your God is with you wherever you go." —Joshua 1:9

"Do not fear, for I am with you, do not be afraid, for I am your God; I will strengthen you, I will help you, I will uphold you with my victorious right hand."
—Isaiah 41:10

Queen Vashti was courageous. Yet, often when she comes up in sermons or Bible studies, she is described as a shrew, recalcitrant, disrespectful person—someone who deserved to lose her crown. It's interesting but perhaps not surprising that she is demonized and cast as a villain in a story that makes Esther the heroine. While it is true that, after being encouraged by Mordecai, Esther saves the day, Queen Vashti's courage paves the way for Queen Esther to step up for "such a time as this" (Esther 4:14).

Consider the Book of Esther. King Ahasuerus had a six-month party for the nobles and princes of his 127 provinces from India to Ethiopia. He spared no expense for the party, which included unrestrained drinking, to show off the riches of his kingdom. At the same time, Queen Vashti had a separate party in a different part of the palace for the women. Following the six-month party, King Ahasuerus held another banquet lasting seven days. On the seventh day, "when the king was merry with wine" (Esther 1:10), he commanded the eunuchs to bring the queen before him wearing the royal crown. Numerous scholars suggest that he wanted her to appear with *only* the crown on so that he could show off her bodily beauty. Queen Vashti refused, and the king was enraged. In fact, the New Revised Standard Version says that his "anger burned within him" (Esther 1:12). The king then consulted his sages about what he should do about the queen's refusal to obey him. They advised him to never see Queen Vashti again and to give her position to "another who is better than she" (v. 19b). He was also to issue a decree that would impact her and all other women in the kingdom, saying that "all women will give honor to their husbands, high and low alike" (v. 20). The letters to all the royal provinces were to say that "every man should be master in his own house" (v. 22b). Sadly, this is still the position of women in some cultures and households even now, both globally and here in the United States.

We can learn several leadership lessons from the courage of Queen Vashti. These lessons require us to reframe her response to the king and what happens afterward. If we examine this scenario in its broader context, Queen Vashti is actually a model of courage, rather than a difficult and disobedient woman. Her denial of the king's request cost her the crown, but she maintained her dignity and self-respect, and perhaps even kept herself and the other women in the palace out of harm's way.

Showing courage will cost something. For Queen Vashti, it was her crown and her position of power. The cost of courage can be anything from the loss of a job to the loss of a life. There are usually no parades or celebrations for courageous actions. No special awards ceremonies or pats on the back. But eventually what is gained will outweigh what is lost. The king and the other men were drunk. They had orders from the king *to do whatever it is they wanted* while the king beckoned Queen Vashti to put her naked body on display for all the men at his party. The king dishonored her position in making this request and didn't consider the consequences that obeying his request would have for her. Possibly, he could not imagine that anyone would harm her, yet he put her in a potential position to be humiliated at best and violated at worst. Seeing a no-win situation, her response, then, was not only courageous but also wise. She did not allow herself to be degraded or dishonored for the drunken king to save face. Queen Vashti was courageous in a moment that called for her defiance. She spared herself and others from mistreatment and possibly physical harm—a courageous but costly decision.

Christian leaders often find themselves in consequential decision-making situations. The response by the king to the queen's courage was unwarranted and impacted all the women of the kingdom. There would have been an impact either way, whether or not she stood up for herself. Sometimes people choose not to be courageous because they believe if they just do what they are asked or told—if they just play by someone else's rules, if they just conform, compromise their integrity, or go along to get along—everything will work out. History tells a much different story. It is the ones who take a stand against injustice or impropriety who change history, upend wrongdoing, and save the day. In other words, courage happens when leaders lead. That is why we recognize that without Queen Vashti's courage, there would be no Queen Esther. Because Queen Vashti was willing to stand up for herself, she paved the way for Queen Esther to also take a stand when not just her life, but also the lives of her people depended on it.

Honestly, being courageous can be daunting. It puts us in a place of vulnerability. There's always a chance that, rather than being celebrated or thanked, the courageous leader is ostracized, berated, demoted, or ignored. It is much easier to be silent, to do what we're asked, or to wait for someone else to be courageous than it is to be the one to stand up or speak out against something that is wrong. Certainly, if being courageous were easy, more people would be.

Courage is often situational, in the sense that no one truly knows how they will respond or decide to act in any given circumstance. We can all hope to be courageous, but we can only count on it to the extent that we are prepared and committed to courageous leadership as a necessary part of our role. To be certain, some leaders have figured out how to show courage regardless of the situation or the people involved. But far too many leaders struggle with courage, especially when a lot is at stake for themselves and for others. Courage is required of Christian leaders, but it is not always evident in their actions.

I am struck by the number of times in the Bible that the issue of fear comes up. Repeatedly, biblical characters are encouraged not to be afraid. Abram (Abraham), Joshua, Jeremiah, and Elijah were all told to *fear not*. Moses encouraged the people of Israel throughout the Exodus and in the wilderness not to be afraid. Deborah pushed Barak to overcome his fear and fight Sisera. The Lord told Gideon not to be afraid, for he would not die even though God has instructed him to reduce his army of twenty-two thousand to three hundred. Esther conquered her fear and pleaded with the king on behalf of the Jews whose lives were being threatened by an annihilation decree. The angel of the Lord told Joseph not to be afraid of Mary's pregnancy. And Jesus let the disciples know on more than one occasion that they needed not to be afraid. Christian leaders should be courageous leaders. We read the accounts of courage in biblical texts, and we celebrate and tout those characters as exemplary. Their stories are examples for us to follow as we seek to be Christian leaders ourselves.

Why is it important for Christian leaders to be courageous? Because, ultimately, God holds us accountable for our actions. This is true regardless of the setting in which we are leading—within the church or outside of it. As we negotiate the spaces between the secular and the sacred and attempt to lead as ambassadors for Christ in the world, people look to leaders as examples whose behavior they should mirror. They expect leaders to be able to make tough decisions but to do so judiciously and with intention. Christian leaders are expected to have integrity and a moral compass by which they lead others. This demands courage and trust in God. Christian leaders who aren't trustworthy because they are easily dissuaded and timid in how they lead will eventually find themselves off course and out of alignment with God's intentions. But courageous Christian leaders model their own faith journey to others by boldly moving on God's behalf.

We must recognize that being courageous is not simple, even when it is obvious that a circumstance necessitates courage. People who are courageous are not always recognized for their bravery by their contemporaries. Rather, in retrospect, we gain a fuller sense of how someone's courageous act made a difference. This is one of the reasons why leadership can be lonely. When hard decisions must be made, it's the leader who must do it. When bold action is required, the leader is who is out front, often vulnerable, and at risk of failure, ridicule, judgment, or being misconstrued. Most of us cannot claim to have been courageous in every moment where boldness was the proper response. But all Christian leaders can learn from the times when they have fallen short or missed the moment.

Tamika Mallory is a cofounder of Until Freedom, one of the former co-chairs of the Women's March on Washington, and a member of my home church in New York. Speaking at a faith leaders' advocacy training conference, she said that if we do not regularly feel nervous and sick to our stomachs in doing justice work, we probably aren't doing it right.[2] Her point was that justice work takes courage. The courage needed for justice advocacy requires going outside of our comfort zones, which is not for the faint of heart. Neither is Christian leadership, by the way.

Mallory's words resonated with me when she spoke and came to life for me a few months later. I was part of a small committee that organized what we believed to be the first Black Clergy Advocacy Day in the nation's capital. We invited clergy leaders from targeted states to come to Washington, DC, to advocate on issues that were pertinent to the most vulnerable in our society. Several of us had decided that the moment called for direct action, for civil disobedience, to offer a public witness that God was on the side of the vulnerable and against any legislative action that might put people's lives and well-being in jeopardy.

I had been one of the point people planning the civil disobedience. When the moment came to proceed, we faltered and discussed whether we should go through with it. At that moment, I understood what Tamika Mallory meant. People were looking to me for leadership and, although I had felt very confident about our planned action, I wasn't so sure that we should proceed when the moment arrived. I was nervous and felt sick to my stomach, just as Mallory warned. People were asking me whether we should continue with our planned action, and I was asking God for a sign to indeed proceed. I was nervous because I wasn't sure how things would turn out and if the arrest would go as planned. I didn't know for certain whether someone might get hurt or something unexpected would happen. I couldn't predict whether the action would be successful in shining light on the importance of the legislation. I did believe that clergy leaders needed to make a strong statement about the gravity of what was at stake by putting our bodies on the line for the *least of these*, but I was not in control of the outcome.

The moment called for courage. As I prayed, I knew the answer was to move forward with our plans. We did just that and were arrested for kneeling in prayer on behalf of the most vulnerable in the rotunda of one of the Senate office buildings, just feet away from the Senate Majority Leader's office. This act of powerful witness received more news coverage than we anticipated and brought attention to the significance of the legislation. We were very glad we pressed through our fear and doubts and that, in this case, things worked out even better than we had hoped.

The issue of fear in the face of challenges or adversity is real, especially in moments when someone's life or livelihood is in jeopardy. As God assured those biblical characters not to be afraid, I believe God tells us, particularly Christian leaders, the same thing. Move forward. Press on. Push through it. Do not fear. Do not be afraid. Courage is also evident in less dramatic but equally important life decisions. For example, do I take a chance on a new job or stay where I am, even though I hate it or it's no longer a challenge? Do I pursue a degree? Do I stay in that relationship? Do I start my own business? Do I speak up on someone else's behalf? Practicing courage in both little and big decisions prepares us to be courageous in the moments that are consequential.

A key to being a courageous Christian leader is recognizing that courage is *countercultural*. Courage means being willing to go against the grain, to stand up, or to speak out when others are hesitant or unwilling. Being the one person standing up and going in the opposite direction of everyone else can be incredibly difficult. But Christian leaders should never fall prey to *groupthink*. This is a term I learned in business school that informs how faulty decisions can be made when the pressure to fit in with the group overrides reason, creativity, or even facts. The dangers of groupthink gained greater attention following the tragic death of seven astronauts who lost their lives in the Challenger space shuttle in 1986. This accident occurred when the temperature was too low for the O-rings on the right rocket booster to work properly, causing the catastrophe.

Prior to the shuttle launch, a few of the engineers expressed concern that the O-rings had not been tested in cold enough temperatures and, therefore, they could not be counted on to work. The culture at the time made it difficult for those with a different opinion from the mindset of the group to be heard. They were determined to have the launch move forward as scheduled. Consequently, the pressure of the group overruled those who expressed concern that the mission might not succeed. What happened in that room was a classic example of groupthink, because the pressure to fall in line with the group outweighed the legitimate safety concerns about the shuttle—with disastrous consequences.

Groupthink happens in board rooms, church and ministry meetings, and other group settings all the time. No one wants to be the voice of dissent, so they bow to pressure from the group or accept the consensus once it becomes apparent that most people disagree with them. Sometimes the group refuses to accept the information or facts that do not support their position. Brené Brown in *Dare to Lead* addresses the hesitancy to speak up or to be courageous when she writes that "daring leaders who live into their values are never silent about hard things."[3] In fact, speaking up and taking the risk of going against the grain is easier to live with than the consequences of the worst-case scenario. Having worked in crisis communications situations early in my career, I know this to be true. The truth always comes out. When it is hidden or silenced, the truth usually emerges in ways that make a bad situation so much worse than it had to be.

The point is that leadership requires courage, especially for those who are working to do anything on God's behalf. This is as true now as it has ever been. Although the challenges are different for each generation, courage is always a requirement. Christian leadership means speaking the truth and going against the status quo. There will always be Pharaohs, Pharisees, Sadducees, and scribes—those who oppose God and the ways of God for their own selfish gain. Regardless of others' responses, or whether it is convenient to do so, Christian leaders are to represent the truth about God in all situations and circumstances.

Yet, it seems as if courage is hard to come by. Whether within the walls of the church or in the public square, courageous voices and actions are atypical. While there is a difference between being courageous and being uncooperative or obstinate, Christian leaders cannot abdicate their leadership to satisfy others or to avoid conflict. Our standards are higher, as we attempt to represent Christ in our words, actions, and leadership.

I remember being on staff at the National Council of the Churches of Christ in the USA (NCC) in the early 2000s when we were considering issuing a statement calling for the resignation of a high-ranking government official. Other Christian and faith-based organizations had already released statements, and we were being asked about our position on the issue. The late Robert W. Edgar was the general secretary at the time. On a conference call, we weighed the pros and cons of denouncing this official, who was a member of one of the NCC's denominations, but who had taken positions that the council firmly opposed. We were under a lot of pressure to come out with statements daring enough to get us an interview on the nightly news. I was one of the people who did not think that the NCC should call for this person's resignation, even though I thought that the person should resign.

After hearing all the comments, Bob Edgar did something that I will always remember. He said, "I need to go and pray about this." He hung up the phone, ended the call, and went into his office to pray. He called me back later that day and said something to the effect of, "I think you're right. We shouldn't issue a statement." He made a bold and courageous move that went against what others were doing and even what was expected of him, since he had been openly criticizing the actions of this official. However, instead of publicly opposing the person, we ended up issuing a statement opposing the official's actions and decisions but not denouncing him—a very different thing. The well-known Bob Edgar certainly could have just done what everyone else was doing and what was expected of him. However, he took the time to discern the best way to move forward and then acted on what he believed was right based on his understanding of how to be God's witness in the world. He made his decision based not on his opinion, but rather on what he thought was the proper Christian response to the situation. I have tried to emulate this type of courage in my own life and ministry.

The example of Bob Edgar shows an act of courage. But in far too many instances, when cowardice wins out, the path of least resistance becomes the path of choice. Christian leaders should not bow to outside pressures to take a certain position, support a particular cause, or do something that is not quite in sync with what they espouse to believe.

In one instance, the leader of a Christian organization decided to move forward with presenting a national award of recognition to someone who was found out to be physically and verbally abusive to his wife. Since the award recipients had already been announced, the organization decided that it would be bad publicity to revoke it, particularly since the awardee had strong ties within the faith community. In another situation, I was at a meeting with other faith leaders, where a member of Congress proudly (almost arrogantly) proclaimed that he believed that Jesus Christ is his Lord and Savior in one breath and in the next said that he supported a candidate who was known to be unscrupulous for political gain. This member of Congress admitted that he just kept his eyes on the Supreme Court and did not pay attention to anything else. He was willing to compromise his Christian values with the hope that court cases like Roe v. Wade, which secured the right for a woman to have access to an abortion, would be overturned by Supreme

Court justices who would vote against it. I told him I would pray for him to have courage. So far, I'm still waiting.

I'm not sure when or how the Christian witness will recover in the public square or in private spaces from elected officials, corporate executives, church, non-profit, and other leaders who boast about their Christian beliefs, but whose words and actions stand in stark contrast to what they profess. Although even the strongest, most grounded leader can experience a moment of timidity, misjudge a situation, or make a mistake, Christian leaders must bear a courageous posture and outlook. The need for courageous decisions arises on an almost daily basis, and our choices say a lot about what we most value.

Learning to be courageous is part of growing as a Christian leader. It's also true that at some point every Christian leader is faced with making a difficult decision where the least courageous choice seems to be the best option at the time. In these situations, Christian leaders must be mindful of their actions. After all, their decisions say something about where their loyalties are and who (or what) they really serve. Paul offers a helpful reminder in his letter to the church at Philippi: "Do nothing from selfish ambition or conceit, but in humility regard others as better than yourselves. Let each of you look not to your own interests, but to the interests of others" (Philippians 2:3-4).

Another significant way that Christian leaders can embody courage is in how they lead. Courageous leadership means having transparency and admitting to mistakes. It means asking questions and respecting the opinions of others, even making room for the perspectives of those who may disagree with us. Doing so opens opportunities for the leader and those being led to grow and learn from one another. It is also how wiser decisions can be made since different perspectives are heard and considered. Courageous leadership for Christians also means being willing to own up to mistakes or to attempt corrective action to mitigate the negative impacts the mistake may have had on others. This is true even when the impact was an unforeseen outcome and if the Christian leader could get away with most people not knowing about the mistake.

Courage means that when we're faced with life-altering decisions, like leaving an abusive relationship, starting treatment for a debilitating disease, or speaking up at a meeting when others may want us to be silent, we press forward and do it anyway. Silence can also be courageous, but it's no excuse for avoiding courageous action. When Christian leaders lack courage, they are setting a bad example for those following them and diverging from the high standard set by Jesus.

Perhaps the most important thing to remember about courage is that *God is always with us.* In each biblical instance when someone is told not to be afraid, there is also reassurance that the person will not be alone. We go on God's behalf, knowing that we are not by ourselves. We can have courage because we are representatives, not the ones in charge. It is God's work, and God can "do exceedingly abundantly above all that we ask or think" (Ephesians 3:20, NKJV). If that's the case, our fears are minuscule in comparison to what God can do in order to help us complete every assignment and every task entrusted to us.

Notes

1. Maya Angelou, 2008 Convocation Ceremony, Cornell University, Ithaca, NY, May 24, 2008.

2. Tamika Mallory, "Where Are We Now? Chaos or Community?" (Opening Celebration, Ecumenical Advocacy Days for Global Peace with Justice, Arlington, VA, April 21, 2017, https://advocacydays.org/2017-confronting-chaos/speakers opening-celebration/).

3. Brené Brown, *Dare to Lead: Brave Work. Tough Conversations. Whole Hearts.* (New York: Random House, 2018), xx.

Conviction: Changing Times, Unchanging Principles

"Leadership cannot just go along to get along. Leadership must meet the moral challenge of the day."—Jesse L. Jackson, Sr.[1]

"He must hold firm to the trustworthy word as taught, so that he may be able to give instruction in sound doctrine and also to rebuke those who contradict it."—Titus 1:9 (ESV)

"Against you, you only, have I sinned and done what is evil in your sight, so that you may be justified in your words and blameless in your judgment." —Psalm 51:4 (ESV)

In his inaugural address, President Jimmy Carter quoted his high school teacher Julia Coleman: "We must adjust to changing times and still hold to unchanging principles." It is widely known in the US that President Carter is a committed Christian and man of conviction who adheres to Christian principles. He even taught Sunday School at the First Baptist Church of Washington, DC, during his presidency. His popularity in the US and abroad are because of his humanitarian efforts with Habitat for Humanity. His work to resolve conflicts and enhance freedom and democracy through the Carter Center, and his commitment to ending racism in Baptist life through the establishment of the New Baptist Covenant has lasted far beyond his service as a public official, which ended when he left office in January of 1981. Washington and Lee University Professor of Politics Dr. Robert A. Strong has said of President Carter, "He has produced an exemplary post-presidency, and today there is an increased appreciation for the enormity of the task he took on in 1977, if not for the measures he took to deal with the crises that he faced."[2]

Congresswoman Barbara Lee, the House representative from the Bay area of California, is another real-life example of what conviction looks like in a Christian leader. She is from the Christian Methodist Episcopal (CME) church tradition and has served in Congress since 1998. After the terrorist attacks on September 11, 2001, America was on the verge of waging war in retaliation. Congresswoman Lee spoke prophetically against supporting the looming war and was the only member of Congress to cast a *no* ballot to a resolution authorizing President George W. Bush to wage war against Iraq and Afghanistan. Fueled by faith and conviction, Congresswoman Lee took a stand that no one else was willing to take. In her speech before the House of Representatives on September 14, 2001, regarding the resolution to support war, she spoke briefly but powerfully:

> I rise today, really, with a very heavy heart—one that is filled with sorrow for the families and the loved ones of those who were killed or injured this week. Only the most foolish and most callous would not understand the grief that has really gripped our people and millions across the world. This unspeakable act on the United States has really forced me, however, to rely on my moral compass, my conscience, and

my God for direction. September 11 changed the world. Our deepest fears now haunt us. Yet I am convinced that military action will not prevent further acts of international terrorism against the United States. This is a very complex and complicated matter. Now, this resolution will pass, although we all know that the President can wage a war even without it. However difficult this vote may be, some of us must urge the use of restraint. Our country is in a state of mourning. Some of us must say, "Let's step back for a moment, let's just pause just for a minute and think through the implications of our actions today so that this does not spiral out of control." Now, I have agonized over this vote. But I came to grips with it today and I came to grips with opposing this resolution during the very painful yet very beautiful memorial service. As a member of the clergy said, "As we act, let us not become the evil that we deplore."[3]

Conviction

I can only imagine the pressure placed on her to change her vote from no to yes. I can imagine the compelling arguments she had to listen to and the many influential people who tried to change her mind, so the United States would seem like a united front amid unprecedented upheaval and chaos following the terrorist attacks. I'm certain some agreed with her position but voted with the majority for their own reasons. But Congresswoman Lee stood her ground and became a witness to the world of what conviction for a Christian leader looks like on a world stage at a critical moment in time.

For her courage and conviction, Congresswoman Lee received death threats, was harassed, ridiculed, and called everything but a child of God by those who disagreed with the stance she took. Twenty years later, the United States was still in an unending war in Afghanistan. When the troops were finally withdrawn, the country rapidly descended into chaos. Congresswoman Lee's words echo in the chambers of time. Her stance, based on her conviction, will live beyond the moment—not because she went along with the status quo, but because she stood firmly on her beliefs.

Conviction is a key component of Christian leadership and is lived out in a multiplicity of ways in daily life. It is the solid foundation on which we stand and from which our attitude, words, and actions flow. Conviction should be understood in two ways in terms of Christian leadership. The first is for us to have conviction about our beliefs, values, purpose, role, and mission. The second is for Christian leaders to allow the Holy Spirit to rebuke, admonish, and redirect them if they are in error.

Authentic leadership requires firmly held beliefs about Christ and what it means to build God's kingdom on earth. For Christians, our conviction rests on our belief that Jesus Christ died for our sins so that we could be reconciled to God. Conviction prepares us to do the work that God calls us to do. Our conviction fuels us to have the drive and passion to be God's ambassadors in the world. It helps us to love God's people with an *agape* kind of love that makes us shine light in dark places.

One misconception people may hold is the idea that having conviction means being rigid and unyielding. However, conviction does not require inflexibility when working with others or when adjusting methods to fit the circumstances or current-day realities. Inflexibility is inconsistent with the kind of humility that allows the Holy Spirit to lead, guide, and direct us. Inflexibility can make it more difficult for us to act on our convictions because it limits our approach, perspective, and creativity. Inflexibility might convince us that things must be done in a certain way, regardless of whether that way makes sense or is effective. Being dogmatic or obstinate is not synonymous with having conviction.

Conviction is also not the same thing as condemning others who do not agree with us. Rather, conviction has to do with our steadfast beliefs about who we are as God's own. It's about our understanding of how we are to live out our beliefs in what we say and do, as well as how we behave. Having conviction means that we are fully persuaded that Jesus Christ is the Son of God and the Savior of the world. Conviction helps us to have clarity and to be unambiguous about our tasks and goals and how we will carry them out. It grounds us, helps us to discern, and make decisions about the way forward based on our beliefs. When we're unsure, our conviction moves us to seek out credible people and information to be able to make sound decisions.

Conviction also helps us to recognize or draw the line in the sand when others are attempting to steer us in a direction or to act in ways that would compromise our beliefs or our integrity. Consequently, when we have conviction, those around us are better served because they can also be clear about the path they are on. Conviction is not a guarantee that everything will go as planned, but it will make the plan that you do have consistent with your earnestly held principles and beliefs. In many ways, conviction serves as a kind of compass that keeps us on course and moving in the right direction.

One of the clearest examples of people with conviction can be found in the Book of Daniel. The book records the account of the three Hebrew boys and Daniel himself, being driven to oppose the authorities because of their convictions. When they were told that they would have to bow down and worship King Nebuchadnezzar's golden statue, they refused. The boys were sentenced to die in a fiery furnace that was heated to be seven times hotter than normal (see Daniel 3). Their refusal to worship any god other than God eventually led to Nebuchadnezzar's recognition of God, as they were not hurt, nor "the hair of their heads was not singed, their tunics were not harmed, and not even the smell of fire came from them" (Daniel 3:27b). The king also bore witness to a fourth person in the fire with them, whom he recognized as an angel sent by God. The conviction of Hananiah, Mishael, and Azariah (also known as Shadrach, Meshach, and Abednego) not to bow down to a false god and God's act of deliverance demonstrated to the king that there was a God greater than he was, and he was humbled by the realization.

Likewise, Daniel maintained his conviction when the other presidents and satraps persuaded King Darius to sign an edict declaring that no one was to pray to anyone except him for thirty days or be thrown into a lions' den (Daniel 6:1-9). Although Daniel knew about the edict, he continued his practice of praying to God three times a day. King Darius tried to find a way to spare Daniel, but with no way to reverse the edict, Daniel was thrown into the lions' den. Yet, in the morning, Daniel was found alive and proclaimed that God sent an angel to shut the lions' mouths because he was found blameless. "So Daniel was taken up out of the den, and no kind of harm was found on him, because he had trusted in his God" (Daniel 6:23b).

The Canaanite woman in Matthew 15:22-28, who begged Jesus to cast a demon out of her daughter, also had conviction. She knew that Jesus could do it and wasn't deterred by the disciples or by Jesus himself. When she threw herself at his feet on her daughter's behalf, Jesus rebuked her, saying, "It is not fair to take the children's food and throw it to the dogs" (Matthew 15:36). She responded immediately, saying that "even the dogs eat the crumbs that fall from their masters' table" (v. 27). Jesus recognized her faith and healed her daughter. Her conviction was fueled by her faith that Jesus was, in fact, a deliverer and had the power to change her daughter's life. She didn't shrink back, walk away, or allow his reprimand to stop her from achieving her goal of deliverance and healing for her daughter.

These biblical examples point to an important truth: God wants us to have conviction. Having conviction is imperative for Christian leaders. It's not just about what we know or what we say we believe. It's also about how we will act on those beliefs as we go about our work and daily life. It's about how we will lead others based on those convictions and beliefs. And it's about what our actions say regarding who we really are and what convictions we truly have. Speaking eloquent but empty words or taking disingenuous actions are not true signs of someone with conviction. Instead, it's how our words and actions align with our beliefs and who we are when no one else is watching that are the true testament to our conviction.

On the other hand, lack of conviction causes disarray and sends mixed messages that diminish a leader's credibility. A leader without conviction is more easily influenced by worldly or ungodly things. Without conviction, authentic Christian leadership is befuddled with equivocation and doubt. Disappointingly, an example of this comes from an international Baptist denomination that changed its position on the role of women as leaders and its designation of another religion as a cult, to fit their political leanings in national elections.[4] In the case of women's roles in leadership, an article on the difference between women's leading in the church and women's leading in public life was sent to its state affiliates to clarify the confusion many had expressed as to why a woman vice-presidential candidate was acceptable. It later changed its designation of one religion being a cult, removing all references to it from its website and in written materials. One well-known and highly regarded evangelical association that is closely aligned with the denomination also changed its designation of the same religion being a cult.

These actions left many to wonder out loud whether the perspective about gender roles and the religion being considered a cult changed for political rather than theological reasons. Would this denomination change other strongly held beliefs for political gain? There were certainly valid concerns about what their convictions were because of the timing of these changes in perspective—concerns that have only become more magnified as toxic polarization in American society has intensified.

Sadly, Christian leaders who do not operate out of their convictions—and those who don't seem to have any conviction outside of their own ambition—are all too common. Consider a leader who, when confronted with facts that refute the narrative want to push, might wreak havoc by telling contradictory information to different people just to get their way. Or consider another who might lie, manipulate, and even bully people to get the outcomes they want rather than humble themselves, admit mistakes, and take corrective action. These kinds of behaviors have resulted in congregations splitting, organizations folding, and relationships being fractured.

When we put ourselves and our own ambitions and self-interests above our espoused beliefs, we demonstrate that we are being "tossed to and fro" by every wind of doctrine and not standing on our convictions. This kind of duplicitousness does not bode well for Christian leaders or for those they lead. Christian leaders are charged with bringing people together, directing and instructing them on making godly decisions, and moving them to act in meaningful ways—not leading them astray. Having conviction about our beliefs and living them out ensures that we are on a righteous rather than destructive path.

Perhaps it seems obvious that Christian leaders should act according to their convictions. The reality is far more complicated. Some profess to be Christians, yet their words and actions are inconsistent with what they say they believe. Consider a pastor who is convicted of embezzling millions of dollars from the church but still doesn't resign while serving a prison sentence. Or think about an entrepreneur who prints Scripture on the cups given to customers but is found guilty of domestic violence. What will people think about a faithful church leader who participates in rallies of hate groups? Similarly, how does the world receive a restaurant owner who demonstrably purports Christian faith but supports political candidates and organizations that cause harm to others? Imagine the evangelist who travels the world preaching Jesus but openly lies and prophesies falsely or the leader of a large business conglomerate who refuses to pay employees a living wage or cover healthcare costs for workers. It is hard not to question the motivation of these leaders and what their conviction really is. Their behavior shines a negative light on all Christians and damages their own witness. At the same time, their actions make it harder for others to reach those with whom they may want to share the gospel. To be clear, if you're getting rich while denigrating others, that's not God blessing you, nor is it authentic Christian leadership. It's greed.

Conviction can also make a difference in the lives of Christian leaders when we are convicted by the Holy Spirit, letting us know when we are off course and headed in the wrong direction. Our ability to deal with our mistakes and imperfections is a sign of our maturity, leadership ability, and effectiveness. We cannot do what we want, when we want, how we want, without boundaries or limitations. We are absolutely covered by God's grace when we make mistakes. However, the words of the apostle Paul to some misguided members of the church at Corinth echo in my ears: "'I have the right to do anything,' you say—but not everything is beneficial. 'I have the right to do anything'—but not everything is constructive" (1 Corinthians 10:23, NIV).

Christian leaders have parameters within which we are supposed to operate. Unfortunately, in too many instances, Christian leaders who have sinned against God and God's people seem to be unrepentant. Consider the church leader who knows his or her proclivity for pedophilia but volunteers for vacation Bible school or to work with the children on the Easter play. Or the person who is tempted by the love of money but is always vying to count the offering or be the chair of the trustees. Or the pastor who told the congregation not to wear masks during a pandemic, knowing that people were getting gravely ill and dying and that masks were one way to protect people and slow the spread of disease. Or the faith leader who lies and manipulates to cover up their own mistakes or to protect their reputation. These are obvious examples and ones that we pray are not happening around us.

However, these kinds of violations and more severe ones do occur at churches, regardless of denominational affiliation, size, racial and ethnic makeup, or location. There are also other offenses that harm the body of Christ and taint Christian leadership. Gossip, manipulation, and spiritual abuse (using Scripture and/or church tradition out of context for personal gain, to control someone, and/or to justify abusive behavior) are other ways that church and other faith leaders can lead parishioners astray. But when a Christian leader has embraced the transformative power of the Holy Spirit working in their life and is convicted when in error, it is much easier to correct those mistakes before they become problems or escalate into church splits or criminal cases.

Mistakes are a part of the Christian's journey. Anyone can err in judgment or make a miscalculation. But for Christian leaders who have conviction and are fully persuaded by the power of God that works in and through us, feeling convicted when our words or actions are inconsistent with God's intentions for us or for other people is a part of our growth process and spiritual maturity. In this sense, the purpose and necessity of conviction for Christian leaders is that it stops us in our tracks and brings us to a place of repentance—reconciliation with God.

Being convicted turns us away from sin and toward God. It keeps us humble before God and constantly seeking to do what is pleasing in God's eyes, not in our own or those of others. Furthermore, being convicted elevates our behavior, actions, and attitudes to meet the standard set by Christ, not by the world. The psalmist says it this way in Psalm 51:10-12: "Create in me a clean heart, O God, and put a new and right spirit within me. Do not cast me away from your presence, and do not take your holy spirit from me. Restore to me the joy of your salvation, and sustain in me a willing spirit."

Notes

1. Jesse L. Jackson, Sr., "1988 Democratic Convention Speech" at the Democratic National Convention, Atlanta, GA, July 19, 1988.

2. Robert A. Strong, "Jimmy Carter: Impact and Legacy," UVA/Miller Center, US Presidents, https://millercenter.org/president/carter/impact-and-legacy, accessed April 25, 2022.

3. Congresswoman Barbara Lee, "Speech on 9/11 attack," September 14, 2001, Washington, DC, US House of Representatives, 2:34, https://lee.house.gov/news/videos/watch/speech-on-9/14/01.

4. Adelle Banks, "Gender debate on church leadership heats up," *The State Journal-Register* (Springfield, IL), September 17, 2008, https://www.sj-r.com/story/lifestyle/faith/2008/09/17/gender-debate-on-church-leadership/41742902007/.

Nathan A. Finn, "Gender and the Vice Presidency," *Baptist Press*, (Nashville, TN), September 5, 2008, https://www.baptistpress.com/resource-library/news/gender-and-the-vice-presidency/.

Barbara Bradley Hagerty, "Despite Divide, Evangelicals Could Support A Mormon," *National Public Radio*, All Things Considered, (Washington, DC), October 12, 2011, https://www.npr.org/2011/10/12/141269923/despite-divide-evangelicals-could-support-a-mormon.

Daniel Burke, "Billy Graham faces backlash over Mormon 'cult' removal," *Washington Post*, (Washington, DC), October 25, 2012, https://www.washingtonpost.com/national/on-faith/billy-graham-faces-backlash-over-mormoncult-removal/2012/10/24/2f9ca0c6-1e1b-11e2-8817-41b9a7aaabc7_story.html.

Commitment: Christian Leadership Is Not a Side Hustle

"You may have to fight a battle more than once to win it." —Margaret Thatcher[1]

"The problem that we are facing in the church today is that we have so many Christians who have made a decision to believe in Jesus but not a commitment to follow Him. We have people who are planning to, meaning to, trying to, wanting to, going to, we just don't have people who are doing it." —Tyler Edwards[2]

"Commit your work to the LORD, and your plans will be established." —Proverbs 16:3

Tennis champion Martina Navratilova is credited with making this observation about commitment: "The difference between involvement and commitment is like ham and eggs. The chicken is involved; the pig is committed."[3] I could argue that Christian leadership is not quite this dramatic a difference, but in a sense, Christian leadership requires our whole selves and not just what we can produce.

Commitment matters. It is foundational to being a Christian and especially to being a Christian leader. Commitment grounds us and serves as a reminder, nudging us along to take the next step on the journey ahead when everything in us wants to turn back or find a place to hide. Commitment is like a battery charger when we're weary or a light when we are lost, in a dark place, or unable to find our way. It is the basis for the other principles outlined in this book. Commitment fuels a call, solidifies clarity, fortifies our courage, compels our compassion, prioritizes care of the self, requires our conviction, maintains our credibility, and centers Christ in everything we do.

Commitment can mean the difference between giving up and pressing forward. As an essential part of Christian leadership, commitment undergirds and drives us to keep moving forward, to finish the race. When we are committed, we look beyond our feelings and emotions, and disregard imperfect and challenging circumstances, while giving our all until our tasks are completed or until our assignment changes. We are *all in.*

It is generally easy to tell which leaders are committed and which ones are not—either by what they say or do, how they prioritize or neglect their tasks, what they deem important, and what they designate as inconsequential and leave undone. Where our commitment lies becomes apparent in the choices we make. For Christian leaders, this shows up in the things that get our attention; how we spend our time, energy, and talent; and how we use other resources that are available to us. All of these actions are indicative of our commitment.

Simply put, commitment is the act of being loyal to something or someone. It is what we are dedicated or devoted and willing to give our all. For many Christian leaders, conflicting commitments are where problems arise. This book's premise is that Christian leaders are committed Christians. As such, being effective and faithful Christian leaders requires leading the same way no matter the setting in which they find themselves. This means whether in a church, corporate/business environment, nonprofit organization, government agency, educational setting, or faith-based or community group, how you lead and think about your role necessitates being consistent. This perspective and outlook takes commitment. It is not possible to take seriously a commitment to Christ while manipulating and demeaning others. While we all have faults, faithful Christian leaders grow and mature in Christ and as human beings. We are intentional about exhibiting humility, patience, and kindness in our interactions with others.

Jesus was not a pushover or doormat. Obviously, some circumstances require a sterner approach to reflect Christ-like behavior. However, we should at least try to embody the teachings and example of Christ in all our relationships and dealings, not just with a privileged few. Commitment to the teachings of Christ, to being a Christian leader, is not easy or simple. In fact, there is an inconvenience about commitment. It prevents you from doing whatever you want, when or how you want to do it—at least it should. Commitment necessitates sacrifice. To claim to be a Christian and occupy the space of a leader means that Christ-like behavior and living should be present in every aspect of our lives.

As Christians, we should be careful not to designate places where we are more Christian and other spaces where we are free to behave in ways that are not a good reflection of our faith. Yes, there are environments where it is inappropriate or would not be well-received to beat people over the head with our faith. I'm not suggesting that we don't adjust depending on the setting we are in. I am suggesting that we not put on Christianity only when it benefits us and take it off when it doesn't. We can also demonstrate Christ-like behavior without ever saying anything about our faith in an I'd rather see a sermon than hear one kind of way.

Additionally, the Holy Spirit's work will saturate and transform our souls if we let it and seep over into areas that we might want to compartmentalize. I don't deny that this can be difficult and not always easy to discern. In certain situations, it can be hard to determine the right way to move forward. But if in most of our encounters no one has any idea about our faith or is surprised to find out that we are actively involved in our church, it may be time to take a step back and evaluate our commitment. It may sound old-fashioned to say that people ought to be able to tell that there is something different about us, but it is nevertheless true. If we act and do everything just like everybody else—including lead—then we should reevaluate our commitment.

It should go without saying that out of a commitment to Christ, Christian leaders shouldn't steal the money. Christian leaders shouldn't abuse people or allow abusers to go unchecked. Christian leaders shouldn't bully people to get their way or manipulate them for selfish ambition. Christian leaders should not be wise in their own opinion, arrogant, or self-involved. Christian leaders should do their best to be above reproach—not because we are perfect, but because we are committed to Christ, the one from whom living waters flow and who died so that we might have life and have it more abundantly. Christian leaders should be authentic, honest, kind, resolved, and resilient. Christian leaders should be open and transparent, not manipulative. And while Christian leaders should be direct, they should not be rude or mean-spirited.

What does it say to the world when those who profess to be Christians do the same kinds of dirt that others in the world do? How can we claim that we are transformed into a new creation when we're not committed enough to tailor our words, actions, and attitudes to align ourselves with the one we claim to serve? For effective Christian leaders, our commitment to Christ compels us to behave differently in every setting, especially the ones where we have the most influence. This commitment isn't only evident in surface ways, like being on time and being conscientious about our appearance. It is also apparent in the deeper things of how we treat people, particularly those who may disagree with us; what we say and do when no one else is watching; how we govern ourselves to succeed in our undertakings; and how we lead rather than bully others to do collaborative work. That means we do not play to the crowd. We are willing to have hard conversations if they are necessary, and we do not fall into the habit of lying to avoid conflict or to cause it. Our commitment to Christ means our behavior is consistent with our faith no matter where we are.

My goodness, this is a tall order! Yes, it is. We who are called to be Christian leaders should be transformed by the renewing of our minds, not conformed to the world. We aim to be ambassadors of Christ, ministers of reconciliation, servants to Christ, God's hands and feet in the world—yet earthen vessels. As Christian leaders committed to Christ, we know that we do not do any of this on our own. We are not left to our own devices or operate out of our own strength. We have the Holy Spirit living in us, leading, guiding, directing, and correcting us. It is our commitment to Christ that is paramount and makes the difference in our living. While we may not always get it right, our commitment to our faith drives us to keep trying to be more Christ-like in our leadership and in how we deal with God's people.

When we miss the mark, we acknowledge our mistakes and take corrective action to fix them. We work to repair broken relationships. We are introspective so that we can identify where we may have gone wrong or where we might need to improve our own skills, even while we assess where others may have failed. Then, we share where things may have gone wrong in love, offering constructive criticism with the goal of helping them to improve and learn from their mistakes. Iron sharpens iron. God has us on a continuous improvement plan, (to use the business term), and it is our commitment that keeps us engaged and helps us to submit to God's plan.

Commitment is important in another way. In a conversation with my daughter's former soccer coach and family friend, Don Blanchon, we discussed some of the challenges facing leaders in general and church leaders in particular. Coach Don, who served for fifteen years as the executive director of Whitman-Walker Health (a community health center in Washington, DC), made a poignant observation. He said that in today's environment, many people are "commitment-phobic," making it hard to get them to volunteer for anything on a long-term basis. Churches and other nonprofits that depend on volunteers must then create ways for people to get and stay involved that only require short-term commitments. This is problematic for the church as well as for faith-based organizations and community groups, both from a *practical* and *spiritual* standpoint. It also means that Christian leaders are tasked with engaging others in ways that they may not have had to in the past, including using social media and new technologies, to attract the attention of multiple generations of people.

A good Christian leader commits to living by God's precepts as understood through the lens of Scripture and through Christ. It is also a collective commitment, experienced through the community of faith. Initially, Christians make a commitment through baptism and church membership to help build God's kingdom on earth. Their commitment is a part of their confession and acknowledgment of faith in Jesus Christ. That fundamental commitment grows and dictates using one's time, talent, and treasure to benefit God's people.

In the context of the local church, volunteers largely do most of the work of the church. Reluctance to volunteer or commit to serve works against the overall goals of Christian discipleship. If those who have committed to Christian discipleship are not also committed to live out that relationship by sacrificing and giving of themselves to benefit others, then they are being counterproductive and making it harder to advance God's kingdom. Moreover, as we think about Christians' living out their witness in settings outside of the local church, being commitment-phobic does not bode well for meeting our goals, making an impact, or positively influencing those around us.

Similarly, it is essential for Christian leaders to be willing to commit to work in ministry and serve God's people. Some two thousand years ago Jesus told his disciples, "The harvest is plentiful, but the laborers are few" (Matthew 9:37a). For those who are called to serve in leadership roles today, commitment is still primary.

An effect of the pandemic is that numerous ordained clergy have decided to leave parish ministry. The strain of maintaining a local church in an unprecedented financial and public health crisis was overwhelming for most of us. For clergy, this has meant having to find ways to quickly adapt. Many began to meet virtually and worked to figure out ways to keep members safe when it was acceptable to gather again in person. Decisions to change employment under these circumstances of overwhelm is not the same thing as not being a committed Christian leader. Our commitment is more about *who we are* than *what we do*. It's more than how we are led to live out our vocation. It's about how we embody and live out the principles we hold most dear to us. Job titles and positions can change as life circumstances change. What should remain consistent is our commitment to our faith and how we show up in the spaces where we are assigned. In other words, commitment to Christ is not a side hustle.

Foundational to leadership in the context of church life is that we serve others, not that we expect others to serve us. The commitment is to do what no one else wants to do, to be in the underbelly of ministry with others, where things can get messy. Despite the numerous Hollywood-style portrayals of ministry, the reality is that serving other people when they are most vulnerable is sometimes unpleasant. Calling on people in hospitals and nursing homes, feeding those who are hungry, visiting those who are incarcerated—these ministry activities reap their own rewards but are not glamorous. When we devote ourselves to the work, deny ourselves, and pick up our cross to follow Christ, God is pleased with us and deems us faithful servants. That takes commitment. In no way does this mean our commitment should kill us—that we serve until it hurts, that we have no boundaries or balance in our lives. It does mean that commitment moves us beyond our feelings, self-interests, or what may be trending and popular at any given moment in time.

It is impossible to be a servant-leader or a Christian leader without commitment and bearing the weight of leading others in ways that improves everyone's lives, not just a select few. Christian leaders are supposed to look out for the best interests and development of others. This is part of the Christian call to love our neighbors and to follow Christ. Importantly, God doesn't expect servant-leaders to sacrifice themselves in unhealthy ways or have a *Messiah complex*, believing that nothing can be done without them and only they can save a person, project, or organization. Servant-leaders are to strive for balance and to be sober-minded while caring for and about the people they serve.

Commitment at the expense of self-care, however, becomes something that borders on idolatry. Being committed is not the same thing as being busy or spending every day at the church or on video conference calls in meetings. A friend recognized that she had spent too much time at church for years. Upon reflection, she realized that she had used the church to fill other voids she felt in her life. Adjusting how much time we invest in anything is part of the self-reflection and introspective work Christian leaders must do to stay on course and to guard from bitterness and burnout.

In reality, the number of hours in the day will not change, nor will the number of days in the week! Most of us tend to cram as many meetings and activities as possible into the course of a day and week. Many Christian leaders fall into the trap of confusing being busy with being effective. When we are overly committed, we cannot give our all to any one thing. Commitment also means discerning where our gifts are most needed and focusing our attention and resources there. At the same time, we can recommend others for leadership roles that we cannot fill. We can delegate when our plates are full.

While balance is crucial, commitment does sometimes mean being present when we don't feel like it and when it's inconvenient. It's coming early, staying late, and filling in the gaps where needed. Christian leadership requires working through uncertainty, unpopularity, and constant change. It means showing up when others are ready to give up or have already thrown in the towel. It's thinking creatively about solutions and approaches that will meet the needs of God's people. It's being engaged and involved in the lives of others to make a difference. It's envisioning and working toward a brighter and more hopeful future such that it will be on earth as it is in heaven.

Notes

1. "Sayings of the Week," *The Observer* (London, UK), January 14, 1979, p. 11, Col. 2.

2. Tyler Edwards, *Zombie Church: Breathing Life Back into the Body of Christ* (Grand Rapids, MI: Kregel Publications, 2011).

3. "A Style of Her Own," *Newsweek,* September 6, 1982, https://www.oxfordreference.com/view/10.1093/acref/9780191826719.001.0001/q-oro-ed4-00012583.

Compassion: Jesus' Superpower

"Our human compassion binds us the one to the other—not in pity or patronizingly, but as human beings who have learnt how to turn our common suffering into hope for the future". —Nelson Mandela[1]

"Jesus wept." —John 11:35 (KJV)

Mary and Martha were upset. Even more than that, they were disappointed. They were certain that if Jesus had just been there, their brother Lazarus would not have died. They had called for Jesus, and he did not come until it was too late. How could Jesus have let this happen? They had been following him, serving him, and telling others about him. They knew that he could heal the sick, make demons flee, turn water into wine, and stop the hemorrhaging of a woman with an issue of blood. Yet, in their hour of need, when it counted the most for them, Jesus did not come when they sent for him. Then, he showed up when it was too late—or so they thought. I can imagine that after Lazarus had been dead for four days, the last person they wanted to see was Jesus. But he shows up and in grand fashion says, "Lazarus, come out!" Sure enough, their brother emerged from the tomb where they laid him, and after having his grave clothes taken off, he sat down and had a meal with them! However, before the shout and celebration, before he performed this resurrection miracle, Jesus heard Mary and Martha's tearful complaint against him, and he *wept*.

I imagine you know the story, but let's consider this moment. Jesus, knowing that he would resurrect Lazarus, who was dead, took a few precious moments sitting in Mary and Martha's pain and cried with them. "Blessed are those who mourn," he had said (Matthew 5:4). Was it the weight of their grief that led him to weep? It must have been. From the time he heard of Lazarus's illness, Jesus had already declared that Lazarus was not sick unto death but so that the glory of God would be revealed. So, why did he weep?

If you've ever been with a family or in a family that has experienced a great loss, you can certainly relate to what it must have been like for Jesus to encounter Mary, Martha, and the other mourners. How could he not weep with them? When they thought all was lost and questioned the relationship they had with him, Jesus wept first and then raised Lazarus from the dead. To the glory of God! Compassion.

One of the great themes and the beauty of the gospels is that they tell the stories of Jesus' compassion for others. Repeatedly, we find a Jesus who does not look away from the circumstances of those suffering or in pain. Instead, he leans into the muck and mire of humanity and meets those suffering in their moment of need. Jesus has true compassion—compassion for the sick, compassion for the widow, compassion for those caught in sin, compassion for the tax collector, compassion for those at a wedding with no more wine, compassion for a sick child and an anxious parent, compassion for a man tormented by demons, and a woman who was a prostitute. Jesus has compassion. As Christian leaders, we must have compassion, too.

To be honest, it's almost as if we could dub compassion as one of Jesus' superpowers. (Yes, I'm a Marvel Comics fan.) I don't mean to minimize who Jesus is with the pop-culture reference. I use it to illustrate how Jesus' compassion is revolutionary and life-changing. The way that he encounters people and resides in their circumstances is incredible. He cares for people in ways that turn their lives upside down and changes *their* circumstances, and he also changes the lives and circumstances of *everyone around them*. Transformation happens because Jesus has compassion for people. And according to Scripture, Jesus now sits at the right hand of God, continuing to intercede for us—showing compassion as he makes petitions on our behalf.

"Be kind, for everyone you meet is fighting a hard battle" is a saying that has been credited to several people. Regardless of its true source, this adage reminds us how we never know what someone is going through at any given moment. Church folks are masterful at covering up and disguising when they are going through a difficult time. Spiritual clichés often mask hidden and deeply rooted problems such as financial hardships, marital troubles, debilitating diseases, abusive relationships, suicidal thoughts, depression, other mental health issues, addictions, and a vast array of other troubles. Sometimes not sharing our troubles is warranted. Not every Christian is able to handle another person's crisis confidentially or with integrity. Some people are just not helpful even when they don't intend to be harmful. However, effective Christ-like leaders are trustworthy and have the compassion needed to be a safe landing place for those who are hurting or struggling.

Christians are not exempt from experiencing trials and heartache. Troubles are part of the human condition. Yet sometimes, some Christians seem like the least compassionate, the most condemning, and the most unsympathetic. Honestly, we must admit that we are sometimes more willing to give advice than to give a helping hand or even just listen to someone else's story. We make many assumptions about people and their situations. Then, we base our responses on those assumptions, which are sometimes inaccurate or one-sided. At times, we are the first, rather than the last, to throw stones at the person caught doing wrong.

Consider the clergyperson who called out a single mother (who was struggling financially) for not consistently giving a tithe to the church. What this pastor did not know was that the child support she had been receiving had been cut in half suddenly and without notice. Rather than find out from her what was going on, the pastor decided to make a point of saying she was experiencing financial hardship because she was not tithing. Perhaps it is debatable whether she should have been tithing, but the lack of compassion or concern for someone experiencing a difficult time is noteworthy and questionable. Effective Christian leaders give the benefit of the doubt as much as possible because most of the people they are leading are fighting a hard battle, and some of them will never say a word about it.

The essence of leading as a Christian is to have compassion for God's people. How dare we belittle those who face the same trials that beset us? Can we be so bold as to hold those whom we serve in disdain? Having compassion for others is an expression of God's love for us. Lamentations 3:22 says, "Through the LORD's mercies we are not consumed, because His compassions fail not" (NKJV). When we embrace God's great love for us and the ways in which God's grace and mercy have seen us through dangers seen and unseen, we are compelled toward compassion for others.

A word about grace and mercy—grace is God's unmerited favor towards us. Mercy is when we do not get what we deserve. Neither is earned; both are freely given to us. One way to look at God's grace and mercy is a bank account that never comes back with insufficient funds, even if we are overdrawn and haven't made a deposit in a while. Yet, because of God's love for us, we are still able to make withdrawals whenever we need to do so. We live off grace and mercy—every day and in every way.

Therefore, Christ-like leaders show compassion and extend grace and mercy to others. We are to be the very first to offer this gift when it's needed.

A good friend of mine, Robin Harris, taught herself how to crochet when her mother became sick. She would sit with her mother for hours, and crocheting was soothing for her. Robin's first project was to crochet a scarf for her mother. When her mother died, Robin continued to crochet and began making scarves for women at a shelter for survivors of domestic violence. She also started crocheting squares as a gift of encouragement for others. On these squares, she attached a note that simply says, "Jesus wept." She sent one of these to me after my father died. This gift served as a reminder that Christ was with me in my mourning, and that I would get through the grief. It also captured the heart of Jesus, who encountered people amid trials and met their most pressing needs. Jesus healed the sick, raised the dead, gave sight to the blind, delivered people plagued by demons, and saved the life of a woman caught in adultery. Jesus stilled a raging storm so that his disciples would not be afraid. Jesus wept.

I believe that Christian leaders are to embody compassion in public as well as private spaces. Having compassion for others in public spaces means that Christian leaders have a role to play in advocating on others' behalf. This is particularly significant in a democracy where we are free to engage with public officials to advocate for just policies with the most vulnerable in mind.

The story in Deuteronomy 10:12-22 is instructive for us in this regard. Moses came down from the mountain only to find the people doing all the things that they were instructed not to do. He then prayed that God would not kill them because of their transgressions. God granted his request and told the people through Moses that God is a God of justice and that they should look out for the widow, the orphan, and the stranger because they were once strangers in the land of Egypt. The text points out that they are to have compassion because this is what God requires and because God has had mercy on them.

The Deuteronomy story is the first place we see the language asking what the Lord your God requires of you. According to Deuteronomy, the response is, "Only to fear the Lord your God, to walk in all his ways, to love him, to serve the Lord your God with all your heart and with all your soul, and to keep the commandments of the Lord your God and his decrees that I am commanding you today, for your own well-being." I love so much about this passage.

The Deuteronomy passage serves as a reminder for us to have compassion toward others. The text is foundational for why Christians are obligated to advocate and fight for others who are dealing with oppressive systems or policies that either intentionally or unintentionally harm the most vulnerable. This is true not because we want to be nice, good people or "bleeding hearts," to use a phrase intended as pejorative. Rather, because God has had mercy on us, we ought to show mercy to others.

Showing mercy in a democracy means that Christian leaders must advocate against laws that are cruel and mean-spirited, and cause unnecessary harm and strain on society's most vulnerable. Our nation has had a history of laws that cause problems for the vulnerable, and Christian leaders must continue to fight and advocate on behalf of those most impacted by detrimental policies and systemic failures. This is not only a civic duty; it is also a *Christian responsibility*. As we engage with our communities, we cannot turn a blind eye to the circumstances or policies that make living out their God-given purpose close to impossible, whether it's irresponsible environmental stewardship, predatory lending practices, *de facto* segregation laws, economic injustice, or other issues.

Knowing God's extensive mercy and compassion toward us, it's hard to understand how Christian leaders can have disdain and show indifference toward those who are suffering. This dynamic certainly plays out when large numbers of people migrate to the US from Mexico, Guatemala, Honduras, and Haiti. These migrants are fleeing situations such as extreme poverty, violence, climate change, earthquakes, and other natural disasters, which make it unfeasible for people to earn a living and take care of their families.

Having been to the US–Mexico border a couple of times, I have witnessed some of these dynamics up close. I first visited when a policy change in the United States had children separated from their parents who were seeking asylum. The entire situation caused outrage and an international crisis. To worsen matters, government officials failed to accurately track the parents and children so that at some point they could be reunited. Horror stories about breast-feeding babies being snatched out of the arms of their mothers as well as photos of toddlers crying as they were taken from their parents were everywhere.

Haitian refugees were also mistreated and terrorized at the US-Mexico border after a catastrophic earthquake caused thousands to leave their homeland in search of food, shelter, and a chance for a better life. Images of border patrol agents on horseback appearing to whip Haitian refugees were a horrifying throwback to the antebellum South, at least for me. My heart was broken by this mistreatment—not because I am from Mexico or Guatemala or Honduras or Haiti, where the majority of migrants were from. My heart was broken because I am a mother with children and can imagine the pain these families were going through. I was heartbroken because I can fathom how hard the decision was to leave their native land to travel through the desert with their children in tow, hoping for a better life and more opportunities in America. I was vicariously traumatized for the children who were torn from their parents and other family members, further adding to the harm and disruption they had already experienced.

I was devastated for these families, not because I had the same experience or had walked in their shoes, although my family history has some analogous stories. I had compassion for their circumstances and showed up, because it was a place where Christian leaders needed to be. I spoke out against the policies because I believe the Lord required this of me. I worked to embody mercy in action and walking humbly with God. Compassion for others drives Christian leaders to be present in the most unlikely and untenable places, not because they've been through the same thing, but because God cares about people in need.

Ironically, during the pandemic, many people who claimed to be pro-life and compassionate toward those not yet born also refused to wear masks, even when it was proven to slow the spread of the coronavirus and save lives. We can only speculate what might have happened—how many lives might have been saved if Christian leaders had been compassionate like Jesus, caring more about others' well-being than conspiracy theories or currying favor with elected officials? We should be able to agree that Christian leaders are to have compassion for all people, especially the most vulnerable.

Certain theological perspectives and ways of looking at Scripture may make us susceptible to being less compassionate toward people who are hurting and in need. Both in our society and in church culture, some believe that if they think positively and do all the right things, and then ask God to move on their behalf, they will receive what they ask for. I'm simplifying it, but this "name it and claim it"2 way of thinking can make God into a spiritual bellhop, at our beck and call whenever we need something. This theological perspective suggests that positive thinking and a checklist of behaviors will make our dreams come true and protect us from deadly and harmful viruses. It also turns "blessed and highly favored," which Gabriel proclaimed about Mary (Luke 1:28, NKJV), the mother of Jesus, into a declaration about materialism! Most readings of this text believe it is about submission and making oneself available to God.

The prosperity gospel may lead people to think of those who own houses, cars, and other material possessions as being blessed, while those who may be struggling financially are looked upon with pity. Similarly, adherents to this kind of theology may think that those who are afflicted with disease have somehow not done something right, instead of recognizing the realities of sickness and disease as part of the human condition. Despite the Sermon on the Mount and similar texts, someone who needs help is rarely thought of by the church as "blessed and highly favored."

Mary struggled with the declaration that she had found favor with God. She experienced heartache and danger for her and her family. There was no room at the inn; she and Joseph fled to Egypt with their baby; they lost sight of Jesus in a crowd and found him teaching in the temple. Mary's blessed and highly favored status did not mean she was on easy street, living her best life. It meant that she had trials, tribulations, and obstacles to overcome. At the same time, Mary experienced God's love in profound ways. She was a significant part of the unfolding story of God's love for each of us and the world.

The challenge is that too many believe that people are poor because they have done something to deserve it. They believe that people are sick, homeless, addicted, suffering from mental health issues, fighting illnesses, overcoming disabilities, survivors of abuse, and afflicted in so many other ways because they are undeserving of God's blessings. There is no way to fully know why someone is going through a season of struggle. It is hardly for us to decide.

As Christian leaders, we should always extend grace and compassion, and offer help without judgment or condemnation. Times of testimony in the church point us to the reality that God is moving and at work in everyone's life, without exception. How their circumstances appear to us does not mean that we have a full picture of what is going on in their lives. Effective and compassionate

Christ-like leadership compels us to meet people where they are and to be careful before making harsh judgments.

Jesus showed the greatest compassion when he died on a cross for our sins. Therefore, Christian leaders are charged with exhibiting compassion for others, regardless of the person's situation. Compassion doesn't mean compromising our beliefs or ignoring a situation when someone has sinned. Instead, showing compassion when someone is hurting, no matter who or what is causing their pain, reflects Christ. Even a rebuke can be couched in love and demonstrate God's grace and mercy toward us.

Perhaps what concerns me most is that often the message from local congregations, denominational bodies, and individual Christians is too often one of reproach, not compassion. For this, countless people have left the church and want nothing else to do with Christians. Rather than lifting up Christ to draw people to him, church leaders who lack compassion end up ostracizing people. Christian leadership requires meeting hurt people in their vulnerability and serving as a ministry presence in their situation. Righteous Christian leadership without compassion is impossible because compassion reflects the heart of Jesus.

Notes

1. Message by Nelson Mandela at the Healing & Reconciliation Service dedicated to HIV/AIDS sufferers & "The Healing Our Land," (Johannesburg, December 6, 2000).

2. Frederick K. C. Price, *Name It and Claim It! The Power of Positive Confession* (Los Angeles: Faith One Publishing, 1992).

Care: "Must One Die to Rest in Peace?"[1]

"Spiritual leadership emerges from our willingness to stay involved with our own soul—that place where God's Spirit is at work stirring up our deepest questions and longings to draw us deeper into relationship with him. Staying involved with our soul is not narcissistic navel gazing; rather, this kind of attentiveness helps us stay on the path of becoming our true self in God—a self that is capable of an ever-deepening yes to God's call on our life."
—Ruth Haley Barton[2]

"Come to me, all you that are weary and are carrying heavy burdens, and I will give you rest. Take my yoke upon you, and learn from me; for I am gentle and humble in heart, and you will find rest for your souls. For my yoke is easy, and my burden is light."
—Matthew 11:28-30

A prominent, well-loved Christian leader was scheduled to do a webinar that night. Many people were planning to attend and were excited about what she would have to say. She was promoting the event on social media herself that morning. Just hours before the event was supposed to begin, those who were planning to attend were informed that the workshop was cancelled, because she had died of a massive heart attack. We were asked to please keep her family in prayer. She was just days shy of her 45th birthday.

Lord, in your mercy.

Shock waves went through the many communities where she was known and loved. How could this happen? Could anything have been done to change this tragic outcome, friends and family asked themselves? *Must one die to rest in peace?*

Christian leaders must not only take care of others; we also must care for ourselves. Numerous studies have shown that pastoral leaders are in the worst health of any of the helping professions. They are generally overweight, overworked, and suffering from exhaustion. It is also not unusual for a pastor to die before retiring from ministry, sometimes in the pulpit (both literally and figuratively). The frantic pace of constantly doing and being all things to all people leads to burnout, poor health, stress-related illnesses, and mental anguish. The pandemic magnified these issues a thousand-fold. The pressure to move most of church life into a virtual space while figuring out how to be present in the lives of parishioners has been a real challenge for most clergy. Additionally, leaders of faith-based and other organizations have scrambled to keep the balls in the air even though there was chaos, confusion, uncertainty, and death all around us.

Teachers and professors scrambled to figure out online platforms and plan lessons suitable for virtual spaces. Essential workers bore the additional stress of staying healthy while being on the front lines of exposure to the deadly virus. Personally, I can attest that I had more meetings and events in virtual spaces than I would ever have been able to attend had they been in person. Certainly, the time that was saved getting fully dressed and being stuck in traffic was all absorbed by back-to-back video calls, conferences, webinars, and the like. It was not unusual to start meetings at 8 a.m. and not be finished with them until 9 p.m. or later. We also lost the art of *cancelling* meetings instead of *just rescheduling* them. With so much of our daily work and school routines online, we didn't even have snow days to take off when there was inclement weather. Emotional self-care when everyone was at home seemed to become less of a priority as everyone scrambled to adjust and survive.

Consequently, clergy and faith leaders, along with teachers, healthcare workers, and other helping professionals, are expected to exit their jobs in record numbers in the coming years. Although issues around self-care and mental health have gained greater awareness in society and in the church, *practicing* self-care as an important part of Christian leadership is quite another thing. I get it. For clergy leaders, it is a part of the struggle. Serving others can take a toll. It's often difficult to reconcile what it means to pick up our cross and deny ourselves with the Godly mandate and physical realities of what it means to rest, refresh, breathe, and pause. It's almost as if we have embraced a rationale that, rather than denying ourselves and picking up our cross, we somehow believe that the God who created us with such precision and genius, knowing we would have to rest, is intent on having us kill ourselves to prove that we are faithful. Not so.

Old Testament scholar Judy Fentress-Williams said that rest is a part of the created order, and when we don't take time for rest, we are working in opposition to the created order.[3] We read about the importance of rest early in Scripture. Genesis 2:2-3 set the stage and let us know that after God had finished the work of creating, God rested on the seventh day and declared it holy. Later, the Ten Commandments instruct us on what it means to keep the sabbath day holy. According to Exodus 20:8-10 (NIV), "Remember the Sabbath day by keeping it holy. Six days you shall labor and do all your work, but the seventh day is a sabbath to the LORD your God. On it you shall not do any work, neither you, nor your son or daughter, nor your male or female servant, nor your animals, nor any foreigner residing in your towns." This commandment sets forth a deliberate way we are to conduct ourselves and order our lives.

Most notably, Jesus also rested and instructed others to do so. In Mark 6:31 (NIV), we glimpse at what Jesus thought about rest: "Then, because so many people were coming and going that they did not even have a chance to eat, he said to [the apostles], 'Come with me by yourselves to a quiet place and get some rest.'" We are commanded to rest just one day out of seven, and yet, we admire people who work nonstop and for extended periods of time. Rest is critical for Christian leaders. It provides us a chance to regroup, gain perspective, tend to our souls, spend quiet time with God, and take care of our bodies. Rest is central to caring for ourselves so that we are able to care for others—and honor God in the process.

The reality is that church life and the work of ministry can be bad for our health, especially if we are involved in every activity, program, and project. For those working in other contexts in addition to the local church, finding balance and practicing self-care can be difficult. I know Christian leaders who are at the church every day of the week and all day on Sundays. Certainly, there are times, such as the Advent and Lenten seasons, when we have to be at church more often. However, being at church every day and becoming overwhelmed with church activities is neither wise nor beneficial—to anyone. Clergy or a ministry leader who must be at church all day on Sunday and therefore cannot honor the Sabbath by resting, choose another day of the week to pull away to rest and care for your soul. Being at church all day does not count as sabbath rest, even if you love being at church. Some clergy will take an entire month off in the summer. This is a great way to prioritize self-care.

With so many Christian leaders opting out of rest and self-care, either intentionally or unintentionally, it's important to consider the spiritual and theological implications of our actions. Is it pride that leads Christian leaders to neglect rest and proper self-care? Is it perfectionism—things must be done a certain way by you and only you? Is it an unhealthy environment with unrealistic expectations that prioritize the work over the individual people (which happens a lot in ministry contexts)? Is it a distorted perception of ministry that embraces the notion that unless you are exhausted, you are not doing effective ministry? Is it a theological issue where one believes God will reward them if they work themselves to near-death since what they are doing is honorable? Is it a misinterpretation of what it means to be faithful? Are we simply emulating what we've seen Christian leaders before us do over and over again? It is likely a combination of issues that hinders Christian leaders from prioritizing self-care, with both individual leaders and churches or institutions creating an unhealthy culture where the expectation is that the one caring for others doesn't get to practice self-care themselves.

Nonetheless, being a Christian leader and doing the work of the church and ministry is *not* a call to be in a perpetual state of mental, physical, and spiritual exhaustion. Serving others is demanding and taxing. It's important to find the right balance and create a community where rest is valued. No badge of honor nor crown of glory awaits the overworked Christian leader. Instead, there are usually health challenges or premature death waiting for us if we don't adjust and become more intentional about our own health and well-being.

Sabbaticals are a set time away from ministry to help us to renew our minds and spirits and to rest from the strenuous demands of ministry. Sabbaticals are a way to reconnect with God on an intimate level. Experts about clergy sabbaticals recommend that they should be taken about every five to seven years in ministry. When Rev. Dr. Howard-John Wesley, the pastor of a megachurch in the Washington, DC,[4] metropolitan area announced to his congregation that he was going to take a three-and-a-half-month sabbatical, he had been serving the church for eleven years. His decision was mostly well-received by the congregation (although some were tentative at first), but it caused controversy in his denomination and cultural context.

Coming from a Black church tradition, it was almost unheard of for a popular pastor to voluntarily leave his pulpit for an extended period. Those who disagreed with the pastor's decision freely expressed concerns about church attendance and tithes and offerings declining. Others commented about someone else possibly "taking" his church or being more appealing to the congregation than he was. All the reasons for him not taking a sabbatical paled in comparison to why he wanted to take it in the first place: he was exhausted and felt distant from God. Recognizing this and having the audacity to admit it was not only courageous, but it was also admirable. This decision was countercultural but firmly prioritized his relationship with God over worldly, although real, concerns.

The rationale not to take the time off for renewal came from a place of fear—fear that people would stop coming to church, that the offering would decline and put the church in financial jeopardy, or that he would be replaced by another dynamic preacher. Fear. None of these scenarios were likely in this situation, and in fact, they did not materialize. Sadly, Christian leaders often allow fear to drive their decisions about self-care. Equally sad is that many Christian leaders, even those in prominent positions, operate from a place of depletion and emptiness because they refuse or postpone taking time to care for themselves. Consequently, their gifts and those they are serving suffer. Their gifts may flow, but in ways that further deplete and exhaust them. These leaders are more likely to emotionally bleed on the people they serve by inadvertently exposing their issues or places of struggle.

When this happens, it's not pretty. I was once at a service where a preacher had recently lost a parent. The sermon recalled every moment of what happened leading up to and following the parent's death. I sat there, feeling the loss profoundly, wanting to run up to the pulpit and give the preacher a hug. But I was also deeply uncomfortable and desperate for the sermon to end. This person was emotionally bleeding all over us, and rather than a homily, we were drawn into their grief in an unhealthy way that left both the sermon and our emotions unresolved.

For preachers and ministry leaders, we do often work out our grief and other issues through our preaching, teaching, and writing. I'm sure I've done this. Yet, we should always be mindful of where we are in our grieving process. It may be that we need professional counseling, to reach out to trustworthy friends, or to talk to our accountability partners. Sometimes we need all the above. Ruth Haley Barton, author of *Strengthening the Soul of Your Leadership*, describes the moment when we realize something is not quite right:

> Such moments come to all of us—moments when our leadership feels like something we "put on" like a piece of clothing pulled out of the closet for a particular occasion rather than something that flows from a deep inner well fed by a pure source ... Perhaps you are preparing to preach or lead a Bible study and you have the sinking realization that you are getting ready to exhort others in values and behaviors you are not living yourself. Maybe you are a worship leader and notice that more and more frequently you are manufacturing a display of emotion because it has been too long since you experienced any real intimacy with God. Or perhaps someone needs pastoral care and you realize that you just *don't care*. You rally your energy to go through the motions, but you know that your heart is devoid of real compassion.[5]

Christian leaders can become impatient and apathetic and, in some cases, cause more harm than good when they do not take the time to care for themselves. Yes, God will fill us up in those moments when we most need it. God does meet us where we are. I am suggesting that it is detrimental for Christian leaders not to prioritize self-care.

While self-care is not rocket science, sometimes it can seem that it might as well be. Practicing self-care can be a challenge for busy and overly committed Christian leaders. Simple things can make a big difference and help us to begin a lifestyle that integrates self-care into our daily routine before we get to the point of having to manage a health crisis. In fact, it may be helpful for those of us who have a hard time prioritizing self-care to think about ourselves as being in a looming crisis: it's not here yet, but it's just around the corner if we don't take the necessary steps to prevent it.

When I was going through the harrowing experience of a divorce, I began to employ a once-a-day, once-a-week, once-a-month method to keep myself encouraged. Every day I would do something intentional just for myself. For example, I would set aside an extra fifteen minutes to sit in a café to drink my coffee instead of taking it to go. It gave me just a few moments to think and regroup after the hustle and bustle of getting the kids to school on time. Once a week, I would do something else that was not as routine as going to a coffee shop. I am a book nerd, so I would go to a local bookstore or the library and spend an hour or two reading and checking out new books of interest to me or that I planned to buy at some point. Occasionally, I would purchase a book, but the point was really to be in a space that I loved and to remember my own value and worth. Then, once a month, I would do something even more special. I would get a massage, enjoy a manicure/pedicure, or go to the movies. I would treat myself to a meal at a restaurant I enjoyed. I would do something that reminded me that joy comes! Spending a little bit of time focused on myself gave me the fuel, energy, and fortitude I needed to get through what was a very difficult time. I've shared this with others to encourage them to be gentle with themselves, especially during a situation that rocks them to their core.

Since getting through that ordeal, I sometimes need to remember to take my own advice. Self-care doesn't come easily to me, so I understand how the demands of life and ministry can drown out any considerations of taking a break. There's really no way around self-care, though. When we do not take care of ourselves—body, mind, and spirit—we will find that we will have to attend to some kind of health or faith crisis down the road. Too many faith leaders end up finding secular work that is perhaps less fulfilling, but also less demanding because they haven't prioritized self-care. In her book *Leaving Church: A Memoir of Faith*, Barbara Brown Taylor says this of her decision to leave the congregation she was serving:

> I had found the perfect parish in the foothills of north Georgia, where there was no excuse for my not becoming the perfect rector of it. I had built a reputation for preaching and writing, both at the local level and beyond. I had done everything I knew how to do to draw as near to the heart of God as I could, only to find myself out of gas on a lonely road, filled with bitterness and self-pity.[6]

It doesn't have to be this way. Recognizing that sometimes *we don't know until we know*, we can still begin to be intentional about our own care and well-being before we hit a personal and professional crisis. We can also avoid burnout by having regular check-ins with a counselor or other mental health professional, friend, or accountability partner.

In addressing self-care, it is important to raise a cultural issue. People from a Black church tradition, particularly women, have a hard time making self-care a priority. This same cultural challenge is in other traditions and family systems where rest is deemed unnecessary and often mistaken for laziness or lack of ambition. While this may not be true for everyone from these traditions, the statistics are clear that it is an issue.[7]

As someone who has struggled with making time for self-care, I must admit that I have believed that "God will make a way" (to quote the gospel song) meant that God will intervene and infuse my exhausted body with stamina and vitality and my mind with clarity of thought and speech. But more often than not, God just wants us to rest. I know how hard it has been to make self-care a focal point. I have even prayed a version of "Lord, renew my mind, body, and spirit so that I can better serve you," but I have prayed it as I went from one ministry assignment to another, taking naps at traffic lights. I have not said *no* when I should have. I have taken on too much and desperately prayed my way through, collapsing into bed at night and erroneously labeling that as rest. I have also dealt with exhaustion and not shown up the way I wanted in spaces that were important to me because, frankly, I was just too tired.

In her groundbreaking work *Too Heavy a Yoke: Black Women and the Burden of Strength*, Chanequa Walker-Barnes emphasizes how the Christian church has been complicit in the myth of the StrongBlackWoman (with spaces between words left out intentionally):

> The church reinforces the mythology of the Strong BlackWoman by silencing, ignoring and even romanticizing the suffering of Black women. Rather than offering a balm to heal the wounds of Black women who cry out about their pain, the church admonishes them with platitudes such as "God won't give you any more than you can bear," and "If He brought you to it, He'll bring you through it."... Imprisoned within the unholy trinity of self-denial, suffering, and silence, the Christian StrongBlackWoman serves as the modern sacrificial lamb, with the church functioning as both the officiating priest and the altar of ungodly fire.[8]

For the health and well-being of Christian leaders and all whom we serve, we must take self-care seriously, and make it as much a part of our culture and traditions as Communion.

Embodying Christ-like leadership means making rest and self-care primary in the life of Christian leaders. Clearly, retreats that are jampacked with workshops, activities, and worship services are not the answer. And although Sunday worship services can be restorative for the individual Christian leader, they are not the same thing as resting. Taking time to regroup and replenish outside of the walls of the church on a consistent basis is necessary to effectively lead inside those walls and in all the spaces where we lead. There really is no substitute. Emerging technologies may make it possible to do more in less time or provide different options for us to get respite, but nothing will ever replace rest. In addition, what we've learned from having a season of depending on technology to replace in-person gatherings is that technology may allow us to do more, but it is not without consequences of its own: burnout, fatigue, and other issues.

Self-care helps us to stay connected with God in ways that nothing else does. Ideally, Christian leaders will take time to pull away from the crowds and even other disciples, just like Jesus did.

Notes

1. Cheryl Adamson, "Must One Die to R.I.P?" (Sermon, Palmetto Missionary Baptist Church, Conway, S.C., Aug. 8, 2021), https://www.youtube.com/watch?v= Y2H5HtkwV3E. This sermon was inspired by Dr. Daniel Black, professor of African American Studies and English at Clark Atlanta University and Morehouse College.

2. Ruth Haley Barton, *Strengthening the Soul of Your Leadership: Seeking God in the Crucible of Ministry* (Downers Grove, IL: InterVarsity Press, 2008).

3. Judy Fentress-Williams, (Bible Study, Alfred Street Baptist Church, Alexandria, VA, June 18, 2013).

4. I am a member of Alfred Street Baptist Church in Alexandria, VA.

5. Barton, *Strengthening the Soul of Your Leadership*, 22–23.

6. Barbara Brown Taylor, *Leaving Church: A Memoir of Faith* (New York: HarperOne, 2006), 123.

7. Alicia Montgomery, "Why Black Churches Need to Do Better with Mental Health Issues," NAMI Blog, National Alliance on Mental Illness, July 20, 2020, https://www.nami.org/Blogs/NAMI-Blog/July-2020/Why-Black-Churches-Need-to-Do-Better-with-Mental-Health-Issues.

8. Chanequa Walker-Barnes, *Too Heavy a Yoke: Black Women and the Burden of Strength* (Eugene, OR: Cascade Books, 2014), 5–6.

Credibility: Show Me the Receipts

"Inconsistency on the part of pastors and the faithful between what they say and what they do, between word and manner of life, is undermining the Church's credibility." —Pope Francis[1]

"Again, you have heard that it was said to those of ancient times, 'You shall not swear falsely, but carry out the vows you have made to the Lord.' But I say to you, Do not swear at all, either by heaven, for it is the throne of God, or by the earth, for it is his footstool, or by Jerusalem, for it is the city of the great King. And do not swear by your head, for you cannot make one hair white or black. Let your word be 'Yes, Yes' or 'No, No'; anything more than this comes from the evil one." —Matthew 5:33-37 (NIV)

I met Sister Helen Prejean briefly, just once. I was serving as one of the staff for the National Council of Churches' Special Commission for the Just Rebuilding of the Gulf Coast. The Commission was established after the devastation of Hurricanes Katrina and Rita in 2005 with the goal of providing the churches and people of the Gulf Coast region with support to rebuild and restore what was lost. We worked to make sure that those who had to evacuate to nearby Houston and other locations would be able to return to their home cities if they wanted.

Sister Prejean spoke at a community meeting in New Orleans. I was struck by her wisdom and how direct she was about the difficult realities facing the people of New Orleans in the effort to rebuild the city, especially Black, Brown, and low-income people. She spoke profoundly that day about the school system and the need for it to be overhauled. She is probably best known for her ministry work to end capital punishment and for ministering to people on death row. In "This I Believe II," an essay she wrote for the book *This I Believe II: More Personal Philosophies of Remarkable Men and Women*, Sister Prejean said something that goes to the heart of credibility for Christian leaders: "I watch what I do to see what I really believe. Belief and faith are not just words. It's one thing for me to say I'm a Christian, but I have to embody what it means; I have to live it."[2] She continues, "The only way I know what I really believe is by keeping watch over what I do."[3] For Christian leaders, what we say is just as important as what we do. When the two are not in alignment, our credibility suffers.

The book *The Language of Trust: Selling Ideas (Products, Issues Yourself, Services) in a World of Skeptics* argues that trust died in America in 2008 after decades of erosion in confidence in "this country's institutions finally reached the breaking point,"[4] and now, we are living in an age of skepticism. According to the authors, "In every place and every issue, the challenge is the same: when skepticism is the rule, how do you overcome the doubt to get someone to believe?"[5] The authors go on to say, "Voters, customers, and even employees look at institutions differently now than in decades past. They challenge your credibility before even listening to what you have to say. They look first for exceptions and contradictions instead of reasons to believe. They assume from the beginning that institutions and people have bad motives."[6] This is also true of the church, faith-based organizations, and Christian leaders. The grace and credibility that was once extended to us because of what we represent as faith leaders is no longer a given. Both in word and deed, Christian leaders must be trustworthy in how we communicate, treat, and handle others. This new way of being is actually consistent with Scripture. Colossians 3:17 says, "And whatever you do, in word or deed, do everything in the name of the Lord Jesus, giving thanks to God the Father through him."

Research shows that Generation Zers (ages 9–24) are skeptical about the church and leadership in general. They don't just believe what they are told by those in authority or those whom we would call elders or seniors. To Sister Prejean's point, *they watch what leaders do.* This is important because it means that having credibility takes more than just having a particular title or position. It means that walking the walk and talking the talk will increasingly be a focal point for effective Christian leadership. It also means that Jesus' words in Matthew 5:33-37—to let our yes be yes and our no be no—have even greater weight and significance. Our youth are paying attention, and they will respond to our leadership based on our credibility. In other words, we need to be able to back up what we say and do with "receipts"—proof that we are being truthful and authentic and that we know what we are talking about. Do you have receipts?

Perceived authenticity is a place where Christian leaders may run into problems. The reality is that the church has taken some hits when it comes to credibility. Even if we were only to consider the last several decades, it is apparent how our credibility has suffered. I would not claim that this is the first time in history that this has happened. Certainly, it seems that the witness and credibility of the church as an institution as well as some Christian leaders is often called into question and, sadly, many deserve the scrutiny and criticism. Whether it is engaging in acts of sexual or other forms of abuse, domestic violence, theft, infidelity, or other improprieties—or covering up for those who have done these things—church leaders' credibility is called into question in a cringe-worthy fashion more often than we would like to admit. In recent years, some church leaders have also garnered skepticism, as they have allowed political power and influence to trump sound biblical doctrine.

Consider, for example, the church leaders who, starting in the 1980s, stressed the importance and preeminence of so-called "family values," only to pledge their total allegiance forty years later to an elected official who represented the opposite of those values in every way. Some of these leaders have epitomized "cancel culture," with their unrelenting insistence that only those who agreed with them on two main issues—same-sex marriage and abortion—could be considered within the ark of safety and saved by the blood of the Lamb. Everyone else was considered un-Christian, wayward, lost, and carnal. The concern I am lifting up here is not about the theology of their beliefs, although I have concerns about what some purport. My issue is how the behavior of those I'm describing has cast a shadow on the credibility of other Christian leaders and the Christian faith as a whole.

Local congregations have been kicked out of denominational associations and clergy and individual members have been disfellowshipped for having departing views on these issues. Similarly, some have fought to keep guns without common-sense restrictions, saying they need them for protection and it's their Second Amendment right, but demeaned those wearing masks to stop the deadly spread of COVID-19 as lacking faith in God. How can guns be needed for protection and safety against unknown threats but masks to protect against an airborne, deadly virus be exhibiting a lack of faith? In doing this, they have contradicted themselves and the faith they purported.

Their treatment of those who have disagreed with them has been harsh even as they themselves began to make excuses for bad behavior, poor leadership, and deadly deception. Sadly, they have not examined themselves or their motivations and appear, on the surface at least, to be following a false god (news reports of a golden statue of a political leader with one man bowing to pray before it has amplified this perception).[7] The major problem with these church and other faith leaders is that they did not just impact their witness; their duplicity has affected all of us who proclaim Jesus Christ as our Savior and assert that we are his disciples.

The credibility of Christian leaders has also been tarnished by persons like the pastor who stole the money and ended up in jail but did not resign from their pulpit, the deacon who violated a child in their care, and the faith leader who abused their wife. Then, we see examples like the ones who repeatedly broke their wedding vows, the trustee who took kickbacks and betrayed the trust of the church, the organizational leader whose dishonesty pitted people against one another, or the director who was manipulative and mean, breaking the spirit of those who worked for them or anyone who would dare get in their way. In all these ways, the credibility of Christian leaders becomes damaged. More significantly, behavior like this is detrimental to those we are leading.

Credibility is hard to build and even harder to rebuild. Credibility is a currency that builds over time and cannot easily be substituted by other character traits when it's needed the most. When a church embarks on a new building or ministry project or an organization needs to raise money to respond to a crisis, for example, the credibility of the leaders making the request will make the difference between participation and disregard, success, and failure. When there is a crisis of epic proportions, like a pandemic, the credibility of the leaders can help save lives. When people make life-changing decisions, the wise counsel of a trusted Christian leader can lighten a burden and offer much-needed guidance, or it can lead someone astray.

It is crucial for Christian leaders to establish and maintain their credibility in ways that encourage and build others up. A pastor-sister-friend of mine, Cynthia Turner Wood, has often said that all we have is our reputation. For those leaders who consistently show themselves to be unreliable, unbelievable, or manipulative, it is much harder to get others to trust or follow them. I used to tell my now-young-adult children that if they want to be trusted, they must be trustworthy. Brené Brown explains the importance of trust in helping companies to succeed in her book *Dare to Lead*: "Trust is the glue that holds teams and organizations together. We ignore trust issues at the expense of our own performance, and the expense of our team's and organization's success."[8] Brown's definition of integrity in the book also speaks to the issue of credibility: "Integrity is choosing courage over comfort; it's choosing what's right over what's fun, fast, or easy; and it's *practicing your values, not just professing them*"[9] (emphasis added). This is especially true for Christian leaders. Showing others in words and deeds what are our values and beliefs is at the heart of Christian leadership and reminds us how vitally important credibility is.

Jesus made this point in his rebuke of the scribes and Pharisees in Matthew 23:2-12. His words are direct, instructive, and hard-hitting but not often quoted or taught:

> The scribes and the Pharisees sit on Moses' seat; therefore, do whatever they teach you and follow it; but do not do as they do, for they do not practice what they teach. They tie up heavy burdens, hard to bear, and lay them on the shoulders of others; but they themselves are unwilling to lift a finger to move them. They do all their deeds to be seen by others; for they make their phylacteries broad and their fringes long. They love to have the place of honor at banquets and the best seats in the synagogues, and to be greeted with respect in the marketplaces, and to have people call them rabbi. But you are not to be called rabbi, for you have one

teacher, and you are all students. And call no one your father on earth, for you have one Father—the one in heaven. Nor are you to be called instructors, for you have one instructor, the Messiah. The greatest among you will be your servant. All who exalt themselves will be humbled, and all who humble themselves will be exalted.

Jesus denounces the scribes and Pharisees, listing in vivid detail all the reasons why they have no credibility and are leaders in name only, concluding in verse 33: "You snakes, you brood of vipers! How can you escape being sentenced to hell?" Ouch! Jesus is enraged by the fact that the scribes and Pharisees are not living up to the leadership roles that have been entrusted to them.

I can't help but wonder if Jesus feels like this about some faith leaders in our time. I certainly strive not to be like them. As Jesus repeats the refrain "Woe to you, scribes and Pharisees, hypocrites!" three times in Matthew 23:23-36, he amplifies the fact that for people of faith, it's not just about having power, position, and a title— it's about operating with integrity. It's about practicing what we preach and living by Godly precepts. This includes the Golden Rule of doing to others as we would have them do to us. The primacy of the Golden Rule is a point that John Maxwell makes in his book *Leading in Tough Times*: "When you manage your life and all the little decisions by the Golden Rule, you create an ethical predictability in your life. People will have confidence in you, knowing that you consistently do the right thing."[10]

Maintaining credibility takes discipline, courage, vulnerability, and sacrifice. It exposes us to the possibility of rejection, humiliation, or both. It's being who you say you are when no one else is watching and making every effort to do what you say you will do—or at the very least letting those depending on you know when you will be unable to keep your word. It's asking for extensions, saying "I don't know" instead of making things up, asking for forgiveness, admitting when we are wrong. It is living out loud by the principles we proclaim and hold as sacred. It's following up and following through.

One pastor who based a sermon on a professor's lecture exemplifies this point. After preaching the sermon, the pastor felt as though she had not given proper credit for the content she had preached. Because of her own sense of integrity, this pastor tracked down the professor during summer recess and sent the links to the sermon asking for feedback to ensure that his work was properly referenced. In these times when people share and copy other people's words and work on social media without hesitation or properly noting the source, the pastor certainly could have gotten away with taking full credit for the ideas espoused in her sermon. Instead, she made the extra effort to make sure she was maintaining her integrity.

Having credibility means being humble instead of prideful or arrogant. Genuine humility keeps us grounded and helps us to not only embody the values we profess but also to operate with the kind of integrity that helps us to sustain our credibility. It doesn't require being perfect, but it does necessitate that we are able to acknowledge our shortcomings even as we continue to grow and mature. It involves a level of transparency and truthfulness that signals to others that we are dependable and can be relied on.

This is the experience of the Shunammite woman with the prophet Elisha (2 Kings 4:8-37). She believed he was a holy man of God, and she and her husband built a room for him to use whenever he traveled through town. Elisha appreciated what the Shunammite woman did for him and asked what she needed. Even though she said she needed nothing, Elisha's servant, Gehazi, told him she did not have a son and her husband was old. Elisha then promised that she would have a son "at this season, in due time." In response to this promise, she asked Elisha not to deceive her. Surely, being able to conceive must have seemed like an impossibility. It's also possible that she had found some contentment in her life and did not want to deal with the disappointment if Elisha was wrong.

Elisha's word eventually came to pass, so when her son took ill and died, the Shunammite woman sought out the prophet. She reminded him that she had not asked for a son and that she had asked that he not mislead her. Elisha responded to her grief immediately, sending his servant ahead of him with instructions to put his staff on her son. When Elisha showed up, he laid on the boy and made him well again. Even in her distress, the Shunammite woman knew that Elisha could be trusted. And he neither disappointed nor deceived her. When she went to Elisha in need, he did not ignore her because he was too busy, charge her for helping her, or ask her to sow a monetary seed into his ministry for her son to be healed, even though the Scripture records that she was wealthy.

Unfortunately, too many leaders would not have taken the time to address the needs of the Shunammite woman. Because she was wealthy, some may have sent an assistant or adjutant to find out what was going on with her. Too many would have dismissed her altogether. This is a problem. God is no respecter of persons (Acts 10:34), and neither should Christian leaders be. In American culture, however, often those who give the most money or have the most influence have priority over those who do not. This kind of preferential treatment is detrimental to the credibility of Christian leaders because it calls their motivations and allegiances into question. Plenty of Christian leaders would have responded to the Shunammite woman or anyone else who needed their help in a crisis. Sadly, the ones who would not respond are the ones who are used as examples of Christian leaders who are inaccessible and not trustworthy.

One major credibility gap occurred when the #MeToo and #ChurchToo movements gained momentum. These movements exposed sexual and other types of harassment in the workplace and in churches across the country and around the world. Women (and a few men) began to tell their stories of being mistreated, attacked, and abused by those with titles, positions, and authority without their perpetrators ever being held accountable for their wrongdoing. Decades of hidden abuses came to light and a revolution began to take place where those who had been victimized were saying "no more." Almost overnight, once-respected journalists, entrepreneurs, athletes, corporate executives, pastors, deacons, faith leaders, elected officials, and others who had been considered effective and moral leaders were exposed as predators and bullies.

The #ChurchToo movement, which began after #MeToo, painfully demonstrated that harassment, bullying, abuse, and violence were just as present in churches, parachurches, and Christian-led organizations as in corporate America and secular organizations. Some strides have been made following the #MeToo and #ChurchToo awareness campaigns, such as employee handbooks and church policies' being changed for the better. However, many church and faith-based organizational structures still lean toward covering up or ignoring misconduct by their leaders. It's unfortunate because the exposure from these campaigns opened the door for Christian leaders to set a different tone and lead with greater integrity. Yet, deeply entrenched ideologies, practices, and theology about how much authority leaders have (even when they're abusing it) have resulted in more shame, corruption, treachery, fraudulence, and an increasing loss of credibility.

Consider the leader who wanted support for a project. In a meeting, the leader reported only the information that would make the project seem viable but omitted information about potential difficulties. The leader garnered resounding support for the project—at least temporarily. Unfortunately, the project was neither well-planned nor a sound financial investment and the organization faced a significant budget deficit because of it. No one wants to find out that a trusted leader misled or manipulated them. If questions and concerns about the project would have been considered, adjustments could have improved the project and made it more effective.

Is excluding important information the same thing as lying? Some may say it's debatable. At the very least, it is dishonest and damages a leader's credibility. I'm reminded of 1 Corinthians 10:23: "Not everything that is lawful is beneficial." Just because you can do something doesn't mean you should do it. Once trust is broken and credibility is fractured, it is incredibly difficult for those things to be restored. The truth eventually comes out, and it is much more prudent for Christian leaders to address issues of integrity when they come up rather than after a scandal exposes them.

In my experience, being over-committed can also impact our credibility when, despite our best intentions, we're unable to accomplish goals or fulfill obligations. Being able to work within the realities of time in sensible ways is important in maintaining credibility. I tend to underestimate the amount of time it will take me to complete a project. This has led to me setting unrealistic expectations for myself and sometimes not meeting my deadlines. When I was younger, I could "pull all-nighters," but that is no longer physically an option (nor should it be). Staying up all night is not healthy or a good way to work. I now do my best to allow for more time than I think I need to complete projects, especially allotting time for the unexpected and for rest. For me, misjudging time and being over-committed have been a constant struggle—but understanding how relationships and credibility can be impacted has helped me to continue to improve these areas in my own life.

Having too much to do is one thing, but not having the skills to accomplish a task that we've been assigned or taken on is quite another. Our credibility can be damaged when we are unprepared or do not have the skills to accomplish a task that we are expected to complete. On the one hand, it is good to get outside of our comfort zones and to learn new skills. What doesn't work is when we over-promise and say we can do something that we cannot do, don't have the skills to do, or are unable to invest the time necessary to obtain the skills needed to accomplish the task or complete the project. This is not about having stretch goals. Over-promising is short-sighted and impedes growth for people, churches, and organizations to only do that which has been done before.

At the same time, our credibility is jeopardized when we promise more than we can deliver or do shoddy work. It's no fun to have such a person on your team—the one who oversells their skills and then can't deliver what's required of them. Christian leaders ought to aim to do things with excellence. Again, a balance must be struck here. As a recovering perfectionist, I know how hard it can be not to "let the perfect be the enemy of the good," as the saying goes. It's also important to know when to let things go due to time or other constraints. However, striving for excellence as a Christian leader helps us to build and maintain credibility with those we are leading. God doesn't expect perfection, but I do believe God expects us to do the best we can. It reflects poorly on our witness when we treat the things God has entrusted to us as if they don't matter.

A word about sex and money—sex and money issues wreak a lot of havoc in the church and faith-based organizations in terms of credibility. Again, as Solomon said, there is nothing new under the sun. Despite Solomon's wisdom and our collective experiences, it seems as if we have these issues on repeat, as damaging scandals around these two subjects come up incessantly. In one horrendous incident after another, we hear about Christian leaders who harm their credibility and undermine their witnesses, because they have gotten caught in a scandal about sex or money or both. Sometimes this results in split churches and diminished impact of their organizations, if only temporarily. Just as bad are those who cover up or ignore improprieties until they become headline news or a social media hashtag. Understandably, it is hard to have a conversation with a leader or friend who might have crossed a line. But not having that conversation could be a thousand times more harmful than speaking up.

Given how frequently these issues come up in the life of the church, it's astounding that we do not see them coming: the relationship between coworkers or ministry leaders that starts to become inappropriate; "borrowing" money from the offering that you plan to pay back; or, having established credibility with the church or organization, making improper financial decisions. Some feel entitled to take what they want for a variety of reasons, including pride, arrogance, covetousness, loneliness, brokenness, unchecked desires, lack of discipline, little or no accountability, and no sense of responsibility. Some leaders have sacrificed so much for the church that if they're not careful, they adopt a sense of entitlement. Burnout, stress, grief, lack of rest and self-care, bitterness, unresolved conflict, and unforgiveness can reduce our discernment and contribute to Christian leaders' falling into the trap of making poor decisions about sex and/or money.

These traps can ensnare any Christian leader who isn't watchful, and all of us are susceptible (think spiritual warfare, if nothing else). We cannot overlook our own areas of temptation or struggle. Being self-aware and knowing our own triggers can help us with this. Therefore, it is important to stay humble and to have accountability partners who have our best interest at heart and whose advice and wise counsel we will heed. As mentioned before, accountability partners must also be trying to live above reproach and adhering to the tenets of our faith. It does not help to have an accountability partner who doesn't hold themselves accountable or who will overlook detrimental, risky, or trifling behavior.

Furthermore, it is important to seek support through mental-health professionals if we're finding ourselves struggling with heart issues that can lead us to behaving inconsistently with our faith. Because of the intensity of leadership, in general, and

Christian leadership, in particular, regular check-ins with support systems should be a routine part of our leadership practices. Credibility is fragile. Putting up guardrails in our lives preemptively, to shield us from issues that are sure to come up in our ministries, is wise and makes good sense. In fact, effective Christian leaders model for others what it looks like to have the support that is needed to stay healthy, balanced, and whole.

Credibility is not just about avoiding the bad. It's also about embracing the good. It's about finding moments to encourage others, as a Christian leader, giving praise and proper credit. It's about telling the truth in love and then governing our behavior in ways that testifies to that truth and shows love in action. Credibility is about caring for others, showing up, and being present. It is about not doing whatever we want, even if we know we can get away with it. Credibility is about being consistent and doing the best we can with the resources available to us. At its core, credibility is about our Christian witness and how we reflect who we say we are and what we believe by our actions. Those who would follow our leadership are interested in what we do. They want to see our receipts!

Notes

1. Pope Francis, (Mass, Papal Basilica of St. Paul's Outside the Walls, Rome, Italy, April 14, 2013).

2. Helen Prejean, "Living My Prayer," in *This I Believe II: More Personal Philosophies of Remarkable Men and Women*, Jay Allison and Dan Gediman, eds. (New York: Henry Holt & Company, 2008), 185.

3. Prejean, 187.

4. Michael Maslansky with Scott West, Gary DeMoss, and David Saylor, *The Language of Trust: Selling Ideas in a World of Skeptics* (New York: Prentiss Hall Press, 2010), 4.

5. Maslansky, 3.

6. Maslansky, 4.

7. Sean Neumann, "A 'Very on Brand' Golden Statue of Donald Trump Is Being Wheeled Around CPAC," *People*, Feb. 26, 2021, https://people.com/politics/golden-statue-of-donald-trump-is-being-wheeled-around-cpac/. Jordan Liles,

"Did CPAC Attendees Pray and Bow to a Golden Trump Statue?" *Snopes*, March 1, 2021, www.snopes.com/fact-check/pray-bow-golden-trump-statue/.

8. Brené Brown, *Dare to Lead*, 222.

9. Brown, 227.

10. John Maxwell, *Leading in Tough Times: Overcome Even the Greatest Challenges with Courage and Confidence* (New York: Center Street, 2021), 122.

Consequences of Bad Leadership: Millstones and Stumbling Blocks are Not a Good Look

"The challenge of leadership is to be strong, but not rude; be kind, but not weak; be bold, but not bully; be thoughtful, but not lazy; be humble, but not timid; be proud, but not arrogant; have humor, but without folly." —Jim Rohn[1]

"Anyone, then, who knows the right thing to do and fails to do it, commits sin." —James 4:17

Consequences are tricky. They seem to show up late but come with a vengeance. They are sometimes the results of our own mistakes. Other times, we have to deal with the poor judgment and bad decisions others have made. Or sometimes, consequences result from issues left unattended. Under bad leadership, people suffer. Too often, the most vulnerable bear the greatest burden. Unfortunately, consequences are not isolated to an individual leader. Consequences also impact those who are being led, as well as others close to them, and those within their sphere of influence. In other words, while bad leadership may come from an individual, the consequences are communal.

When a pastor embezzles money from the church and goes to jail, for example, the entire congregation suffers from broken trust and betrayal. Members of the congregation are also humiliated within the broader community and often must respond to questions about what happened. Stereotypes about pastors using offerings to get rich are reinforced, and a congregation of believers at various stages in their Christian walk are left wounded, wondering, and without a trusted leader. They become less likely to trust the next person who assumes the leadership position, which can lead to conflict from the outset.

Bad leadership is not just one action, idea, or poor choice. This is particularly true because no leader is perfect, and everyone has blind spots. Good leaders can make bad decisions, and bad leaders can make good ones. Bad leadership, then, is a way of leading that does not consider or attend to the needs of those they are leading. Bad leadership occurs when self-involved leaders elevate themselves and strive to win at the expense of others and without concern for the long-term. It's when leaders make decisions that advance their own self-interests instead of the interests of others who will equally feel the impact of the outcome. Bad leadership involves decisions that betray the trust of those being led to advance a personal agenda. It's the behaviors, attitudes, and practices that tear people down, demoralize them, are deceptive, spur unhealthy competition, pit people against each other, otherwise malign people, or detract from the God-given potential and purpose of those being led. A bad leader may have a lofty title but lacks the vision, wisdom, or insight to back it up.

God takes seriously the role of leaders within the community of faith as well as in the broader community. Scripture is replete with warnings of the consequences of poor leadership. Leaders are instructed on how to lead and how to treat those they are leading. Consider the following examples. Jesus instructs the disciples that in order to lead, they must serve: "But not so with you; rather the greatest among you must become like the youngest, and the leader like one who serves" (Luke 22:26). Similarly, Paul told the elders in the church at Ephesus, "Keep watch over yourselves and over all the flock, of which the Holy Spirit has made you overseers, to shepherd the church of God that he obtained with the blood of his own Son" (Acts 20:28). In 1 Peter 5:1b-4, the apostle Peter directs the early church elders to take care of those following them, saying, "I exhort the elders among you to tend the flock of God that is in your charge, exercising the oversight, not under compulsion but willingly, as God would have you do it—not for sordid gain but eagerly. Do not lord it over those in your charge, but be examples to the flock. And when the chief shepherd appears, you will win the crown of glory that never fades away."

Scripture also warns that there will be consequences for those who do wrong. In Matthew 18:6-7, Jesus warns the disciples about those who are in positions of authority leading those under their care astray: "If any of you put a stumbling block before one of these little ones who believe in me, it would be better for you if a great millstone were fastened around your neck and you were drowned in the depth of the sea. Woe to the world because of stumbling blocks! Occasions for stumbling are bound to come, but woe to the one by whom the stumbling block comes!" This holds true for leaders regardless of where they lead: "Anyone who does wrong will be repaid for their wrongs, and there is no favoritism" (Colossians 3:25, NIV). The fundamental question for leaders is, Are we attentive to how these Scriptures apply to our leadership, and what hinders us from seeing how they relate to our lives?

Bad leadership can present itself in numerous ways. When Christian leaders are shady, duplicitous, dishonest, or contentious, divisions result in the church or organization. These behaviors can also fracture relationships in ways that are hard to repair. The tendency to lead in ways that sew discord between those we are leading is problematic—contrary to how Christians should lead and detrimental to the church or organization. Instead, Christian leaders ought to be intentional about bringing people together so that each person's gifts are honored. Leaders should not foster a breeding ground for competition, backstabbing, and dissension. While disagreements may arise, faithful Christian leaders strive to build up the people around them so that they know how to celebrate the gifts of others, even while they are nurturing and developing their own.

On the other hand, conflict-avoidance is also problematic for Christian leaders. It may seem harmless (or even ideal) for conflict to be avoided whenever possible. Most people don't like conflict. But when leaders avoid addressing issues that need to be confronted—whether they are someone's harmful words, attitude, or actions—the inaction impacts everyone around them.

Unresolved conflict makes it difficult for people to work together and to meet shared goals. Like yeast, unaddressed problems grow and expand, casting a shadow on the effectiveness of the leader who allows it. According to John C. Maxwell, "Patience is a virtue in problem solving if you are at the same time doing all that you can to fix the situation. It is not a virtue if you are simply waiting, hoping that the problem will solve itself or just go away."[2]

Consider the pastor who instead of addressing issues within a ministry, starts a new ministry, gives it a different name and new leader, and takes on similar tasks as the "problem ministry." This may cause confusion about which ministry was responsible for the work that needed to get done and who was responsible for doing it. Effective Christian leaders recognize and practice telling the truth in love. Skilled, faithful leaders learn how to offer guidance and correction without tearing someone down, crushing their spirit, or allowing inappropriate behavior to go unchecked. "Problems demand that we pay them attention. Why? Because left alone they almost always get worse," says Maxwell.[3]

Churches and organizations with bad leadership witness the consequences play out in declining participation, financial difficulties, apathy, and disregard for the growth (not just numerical) and well-being of the group. Bad leadership also has physical, emotional, and spiritual consequences for leaders, in addition to those they are leading. Stress-related illnesses are a part of the hidden costs of bad leadership, including depression, anxiety, insomnia, weight changes, fatigue, lack of interest, and other health issues. Unhealthy environments exacerbate these issues, deepening the dysfunction that happens under bad leadership and negatively influencing how those being led work together. Emotional and physical stress make it even harder to negotiate the challenges of leadership, making it even more crucial that Christian leaders prepare, train, and equip themselves to be good leaders from the inside out.

The spiritual impact of bad leadership can also not be overlooked or underestimated, especially because of the injury that happens to those impacted by it. The spiritual toll that poor Christian leaders have on those they lead is also deep-rooted and profound. Bad leadership can negatively impact someone's prayer life, spiritual growth, and relationship with God. It can cloud our vision, clarity, and discernment. Bitterness, unforgiveness, strife, dissensions, jealousy, factions, anger, arguments, and other issues can take root. Unchecked, bad leadership practices can make it easier to sin and to have a reprobate mind. These issues not only fracture our relationships with one another, but they also affect our relationship with God.

Leaders whose behavior in private is not consistent with their professed beliefs or their public persona can also negatively impact those whom they are leading, even resulting in their mimicking the questionable behavior. Those who lead with unrealistic and unexpressed expectations can unfairly cause those they are leading to question their call, purpose, gifts, and potential, taking them off track instead of helping them to be all that God intends. Leaders who mistreat those with less authority than they have also cause harm and sow seeds of resentment. Ultimately, Christian leaders must follow God and the leading of the Spirit, not make an idol out of a person above them, even if that person has a role in their spiritual journey. Guarding against the physical, emotional, and spiritual consequences of bad leadership is a part of the stewardship that leaders have over those they are leading and for which they will be held accountable.

Certainly, Christian leaders benefit from doing their own internal work to avoid perpetuating bad habits and causing problems that will take years to undo. Parker Palmer, in his book *Let Your Life Speak: Listening for the Voice of Vocation*, notes the difficulty of leading from within:

> Leadership is hard work for which one is regularly criticized and rarely rewarded, so it is understandable that we need to bolster ourselves with positive thoughts. But by failing to look at our shadows, we feed a dangerous delusion that leaders too often indulge: that our efforts are always well intended, our power is always benign, and the problem is always in those difficult people whom we are trying to lead![4]

Christian leaders who operate out of their own brokenness often hurt others. Yes, hurt people hurt people. When a leader is believed to be trustworthy but is not, it can cause immeasurable damage for those they are leading if they have not dealt with their own issues.

If a Christian leader is a poor communicator but gets angry when they are misunderstood, or someone is unable to read their mind because they haven't expressed their expectations, problems and hurt feelings can arise. When a Christian leader has a hard time accepting feedback or is unable to deal with people who may not always agree with them, working with that person can be grueling, resulting in misunderstandings, frustration, anger, and bruised egos. There are many possible scenarios, but it is important to be mindful that Christian leaders often lead people who are vulnerable in one way or another. Because of the vulnerability of their followers, leaders can potentially wound those they are leading. Some people require years of therapy to recover from the kind of hurt wielded by trusted Christian leaders. Some have made the decision to leave the church and faith-based organizations altogether.

Still, some people emulate these bad leadership practices in all the wrong ways. Sadly, too many people have experienced Christian leaders who have left them feeling badly about the church and about Jesus. Some believers may even begin to doubt, to question God, and to mistrust their own purpose because of the shortcomings of a Christian leader, believing God elevated that leader to a particular position. While no one can fully anticipate how their leadership may negatively impact someone else, responsible Christian leaders undertake internal work through therapy, spiritual coaching, or Christian counseling. Engaging in internal work results in leaders being the best, most whole version of themselves possible. Anything less means the leader is limping along, spreading their own brand of hurt in those who are following them. When we do the internal and external work to embody Christian principles and lead with those principles in mind, we are best able to lead in the way God has called us.

Most people do not start with bad intentions. Instead, the demands of leadership can result in a set of circumstances that foster poor decision making or carelessness. When we are overworked, missing wise counsel, holding competing priorities, and trying to do everything ourselves, our judgment can be off. Then, we're more likely to make mistakes—sometimes big ones. This is why we need guardrails in place to protect ourselves against the foreseeable challenges that come with leadership. We are better equipped to deal with the temptations and pitfalls that so easily beset Christian leaders when we are humble enough to recognize that it could also happen to us.

No one is exempt from dealing with temptations or for falling into the trappings of having a measure of power and authority. The cautionary tales and warnings from others are real. If we think it would never happen to us, or we would never do this or that, we will likely miss the warning signs that we are headed for trouble. Proverbs 16:18 says, "Pride goes before destruction, and a haughty spirit before a fall." And James 4:6 reminds us that "God opposes the proud, but gives grace to the humble." Pride doesn't just show up in overly confident Christian leaders. It also makes an appearance when we overestimate our own ability to resist the entice-ments that befall others. Obviously, not everyone is tempted by the same things, but everyone is tempted by something.

Note: while most people don't have bad intentions, some do. As Christian leaders, we are to be as wise as serpents, yet as gentle as doves as it pertains to the jokers in our midst. "Beware of false prophets, who come to you in sheep's clothing but inwardly are ravenous wolves," Jesus warns in Matthew 7:15. He continues to say we will know them by their fruit. It is crucial for Christ-like leaders to be discerning about the people we associate with and to whom we give our support. We want to be clear, to the extent pos-sible, about the motivations and heart of those we make space for along our spiritual journey.

If someone doesn't have a heart for God's people or is driven by selfish ambition, then our responsibility is to figure out what our role is in that person's life and respond accordingly. I once thought a min-ister at my church was a close friend and accountability partner. As we journeyed together, I realized that the person was not as spiritu-ally or emotionally mature as I initially thought. Further, their moti-vations in ministry were out of sync with my own. Another time, I found out that someone was using my name and connections without my knowledge to open doors for a project they were working on. Had the person asked, I would have been happy to help, but the way they handled the situation spoke volumes about their intentions and the way they operate. In both cases, I had to confront the people about their behavior and adjust my own to account for where they were on their spiritual journeys, which was not where I had hoped they were nor wanted them to be.

It is critical to have trusted mentors, friends, and accountability partners who are actively a part of our lives. A robust and disciplined prayer life is crucial for Christian leaders, as it is to practice all the spiritual disciplines. Growing and maturing in our relationship with God is one way to avoid bad leadership practices. It is no understatement to say that effective Christian leaders not only depend on their skills, talents, training, and gifts; they are also dependent on God as they seek to lead God's people in whatever setting they find themselves. And the work to mature spiritually continues until our last breath.

Some leaders reach a certain status or threshold and stop learning and growing; they seem to think they have learned all there is to know about leading. However, having been involved in a successful ministry does not necessarily indicate a person has been a good or faithful leader. When bad leadership happens, we can lose our title, position, authority, influence, reputation, and all that we've worked to achieve. Unfortunately, sometimes these losses can also occur when sound leadership has taken place. The good news is that God is a restorer of these earthly matters. The key is for us to attend to our spiritual selves and our relationship with God. When we are attuned in our spiritual lives, we can watch all the other issues fall into place in an all-things-work-together-for-good kind of way. In *Strengthening the Soul of Your Leadership*, Ruth Haley Barton points out that spiritual leaders require spiritual sustenance and nurture for their own lives to be capable of leading others:

They need us to keep searching for the bread of life that feeds our own souls so that we can guide them to places of sustenance for *their* own souls. Then, rather than offering the cold stone of past devotionals, regurgitated apologetics or someone else's musings about the spiritual life, we will have bread to offer that is warm from the oven of our intimacy with God.[5]

Christian leaders can prevent bad leadership practices by crafting and implementing certain strategies. Being attentive to problems, doing our own internal work, being mindful of how we're treating others, surrounding ourselves with accountability partners and people who will tell us the truth in love, and tending to and guarding our own spiritual growth and relationship with God are all tools that Christian leaders have in their toolboxes. Effective Christian leaders are also lifelong learners and always open to God nudging us to lead and be led in ways that we have not been previously. Christ-like leaders embrace a leadership style that is dynamic and agile so that we do not become a stumbling block for those we are leading.

Throughout this book, I've given examples of the consequences of bad leadership. In this chapter, I have delved deeper into those consequences. In the worst of crisis situations, people may die (the pandemic, missing the warning signs of spousal abuse or suicide, or the tragic deaths of those who followed David Koresh or Jim Jones, for example). Christian leaders are rarely faced with life-and-death situations in the same way that medical professionals are. But in many ways, leadership can make a difference in the life of a congregation or organization and in the spiritual lives of those we encounter. The point is that bad leadership is not without consequences for the leaders and especially for those they're leading. It is imperative for us to keep this reality at the forefront of our leadership and to factor in the consequences when making decisions and leading others. While we cannot control consequences that come from missteps, we can prepare and equip ourselves to be the best leaders we can be to avoid, or at least minimize, the consequences altogether.

Notes

1. Jim Rohn, "The Qualities of Skillful Leadership," Ezine @rticles, Jan. 25, 2005, https://ezinearticles.com/?The-Qualities-of-Skillful-Leadership&id=11133——.

2. Maxwell, *Leading in Tough Times*, 80.

3. Maxwell, *Leading in Tough Times*, 80.

4. Parker Palmer, *Let Your Life Speak: Listening for the Voice of Vocation* (San Francisco: Jossey-Bass, 2000), 79.

5. Barton, *Strengthening the Soul of Your Leadership*, 29.

Cultivating Christian Leadership: Some Plant, Some Water

"I have always thought [that] what is needed is the development of people who are interested not in being leaders as much as in developing leadership Among other peoples." —Ella Baker, civil rights leader[1]

"I am because we are."—Ubuntu South African proverb[2]

"Being confident of this very thing, that He who has begun a good work in you will complete *it* until the day of Jesus Christ." —Philippians 1:6 (NKJV)

We were spending time in Salley, South Carolina, where my mom grew up. It must have before 1978 because my grandfather was there, and he died in February of that year. There wasn't a lot to do in Salley, so we kids made up games to keep ourselves entertained. One day, for some reason, I decided that I was going to try to smoke a cigarette. At the time, many of the adults in my family smoked, and I decided I wanted to try it. I'm not sure what in the world made me decide to do this, because I knew it was wrong and that I would be in trouble if I got caught. I'm not sure where my sister was; we were almost always together—but not in this wayward moment.

I went into my cousin's car and took a cigarette butt out of the ashtray. I pushed in the lighter in the car and waited for it to heat up. As soon as I started to light the cigarette, my older cousin, Cynthia, came from out of nowhere and told me to put the cigarette down and not to put it in my mouth. She was angry. I was embarrassed and shocked! I did what she said and prayed that she wouldn't tell my parents. You see, although Cynthia is my aunt's daughter and my grandparents' oldest grandchild, she grew up more with my mom and aunts and is about twenty years older than me. My first cousins and I have a special relationship to this day, and we all had an unspoken solidarity to cover for each other with our parents when we did something a little risky.

Still, I was unsure where Cynthia would land on this one. Well, you guessed it. Not only did she tell my parents—she also told my grandparents! Here I was, a goody two-shoes who was an excellent student and never got into trouble, being called out for trying to do something that was dangerous and illegal. This was not going to go well! I was summoned into the living room to account for my misdeed. Surely, the earth would swallow me whole so I would not have to sit there and endure this humiliation! That did not happen. My father took the lead on ensuring that my embarrassment would not soon go away. There were a few "I can't believe you did that" statements from my mother, and the look of disappointment from her and my grandparents stayed with me for a long time. The truth is that, even though I was furious with my cousin for telling on me and breaking our code, I knew she had done the right thing. I learned a priceless life lesson that day: You must be a person with character even when you think no one is watching.

I recount this incident in my own life to illuminate the point that leadership is cultivated before the first training, workshop, class, or book on the topic. I remembered this incident, which I haven't thought about in years, as I reflected on the things that have cultivated Christian leadership in my own life—and learning that *character matters* has been one of the most important. My cousin's actions also taught me that sometimes you must make the hard decision to expose bad behavior even when you could just as easily ignore it. Her act of love for me was to call out my poor choice instead of covering it up. She let me face the consequences of my actions. It really was for my own good that she told on me. I don't know what would have happened if my cousin had not caught me or told the rest of the family, but I do know that she helped me to realize that my actions affect more than just me. I am accountable to others, especially those who care about and for me.

Responsible Christian leaders seek and obtain the leadership skills and training they need to be successful leaders. Learning how to communicate, run an effective meeting, encourage, and inspire others, and plan to meet shared goals and objectives are all a part of developing good leadership skills. At the same time, developing the heart and character traits of a Christian leader is equally as important. Cultivating Christian leaders means

- modeling sound, authentic, principled Christian leadership in words and actions;
- instructing those who are following on the principles and practices of Christian leadership;
- training new and emerging Christian leaders in leadership development skill sets they will need;
- equipping and preparing Christian leaders for the journey ahead, including what their expectations should be as they negotiate leading others in various settings;

■ correcting behaviors, practices, and attitudes that are contrary to Christ-like leadership;

■ advising Christian leaders on how to negotiate the difficult and challenging circumstances that they will have to confront;

■ Giving and receiving feedback as a necessary and vital part of developing as a Christian leader; and,

■ making space for opportunities for new and emerging Christian leaders to get experience leading others.

Christian leaders are attentive to how they are cultivating leadership in others, even as they tend to their own leadership development. Cultivating Christian leaders is an investment that takes time and effort. As a community of faith, we have a responsibility to one another to nurture, equip, and train the next generation of Christian leaders. For this reason, the type of leadership that is exhibited is crucial and must embody Christ. Indeed, one of the most significant ways to cultivate Christian leadership is to model for the next generation what it looks like—not just on paper—but up close, live, and in color. In some instances, new leaders are charged with undoing generations of bad leadership practices. In these cases, we can start by checking in with ourselves to ensure that we are embodying Christ-like behaviors and attitudes in our leadership. John Maxwell frames this as going from being trained leaders to being "transformational leaders." In his book *Leadershift: The 11 Essential Changes Every Leader Must Embrace*, Maxwell asserts that he became a transformational leader after a tragedy in his life.

> I resolved to become a different kind of leader—someone different from who I had been up to that time. Thankfully my heart was changed, and my actions started following my heart. I became a person who valued other people and

demonstrated that through my leadership decisions, which made others my top priority.[3]

Christian leaders are in the business of positive transformation. As such, our style of leading, attitude, and actions ought to show it in public as well as in private.

While some people may seem to be natural leaders, it is important for churches, Christian organizations, and Christian leaders to be intentional about engaging in the hard work of nurturing, encouraging, and opening up opportunities for leadership skills to be developed in others. Being deliberate about cultivating Christian leadership skills means incorporating the development of those skills into every aspect of the work. Leadership development is a necessary part of an organization's goals, objectives, and strategic vision, including succession planning for transitions in leadership. But as Maxwell asserts, and as this book contends, good leadership takes more than simply being trained. It requires transformation. Christian leadership is a way of being, of embodying Christ in how we lead. Christ-like leadership calls us to lead and to measure success differently than the world does. Romans 12:2 says, "Do not be conformed to this world, but be transformed by the renewing of your minds, so that you may discern what is the will of God—what is good and acceptable and perfect." Our minds and hearts must be transformed, which means that discipleship is at the core of cultivating Christian leadership.

Jesus provides insight into how leadership and discipleship go hand in hand. He invested time to train and equip his disciples for leadership in spreading the good news that the kingdom of God has come near. The Gospels (Matthew 10, Mark 6, Luke 10) record the instructions Jesus gave to his disciples when sending them out. He painted a picture for them that for those who followed him, the road would not be easy. He let them know that they wouldn't have much help ("the harvest is plentiful, but the laborers are few"), and he was sending them out like lambs into the midst of wolves. He also told them to travel in pairs, and not to take anything with them.[4] He instructed them to be able to recognize with whom they were to engage and what they were to do and say whether they were welcomed or not. Whenever they were not welcomed in a town, Jesus said, "shake off the dust from your feet as you leave that house or town" (Matthew 10:14). He told them how they were to receive payment (in meals, according to Matthew 10:10 and Luke 10:7), as well as how they were to help the people in the towns where they traveled: curing the sick, casting out demons, cleansing lepers, and raising the dead.

As their leader, Jesus made sure they had the right frame of mind, knew what to expect, knew their assignment, and how it was to be carried out. He did not leave them to wonder; he equipped them with what they needed to know in order to carry out the mission that was entrusted to them. They also didn't just go willy-nilly into the streets because they were gifted and knew people. They humbled themselves to be taught what to do before going out and witnessing to others.

Discipleship is an essential part of cultivating Christian leaders. As our faith grows and matures, we are being transformed into the image and likeness of Christ, making it easier for us to then exhibit Christ-like leadership. It seems simple but requires a lot of work. Christ-like leadership takes dedication, fortitude, and resolve for both those discipling and those being discipled. Discipling new Christ-like leaders requires going beyond the surface and doing a deeper dive so that mind, spirit, body, and soul are tended to and nurtured.

Yet, we cannot teach what we've never been taught. We cannot help others to grow and mature if *we* are not growing and maturing. While Sunday school classes continue to decline in many churches, other opportunities for discipleship, learning, and deepening our faith remain the heartbeat of churches. Christian leaders are also intentional about finding creative ways to ensure that discipleship happens. Additionally, Christian leaders are committed to continuously learning and growing, lest we become stagnant. Stagnation negatively impacts both our faith and leadership. But the impact doesn't end with us. It can extend to those we are leading, as well as into the spaces and places where our leadership is needed most.

Christian leaders, churches, and faith-based organizations are responsible for cultivating leaders capable of picking up the baton and continuing the mission, while charting new paths along the way. This means, not only do they have to have skills, but they also must have heart. Part of our assignment as Christians is to invest in the growth and development of one another. Our investment into others is an outgrowth of our love and care for each other's well-being. Ephesians 4:11-13, 15-16 brings clarity to our understanding of the different roles each of us plays as they all work together for the edification of the whole:

> The gifts he gave were that some would be apostles, some prophets, some evangelists, some pastors and teachers, to equip the saints for the work of ministry, for building up the body of Christ, until all of us come to the unity of the faith and of the knowledge of the Son of God, to maturity, to the measure of the full stature of Christ…. But speaking the truth in love, we must grow up in every way into him who is the head, into Christ, from whom the whole body, joined and knit together by every ligament with which it is equipped, as each part is working properly, promotes the body's growth in building itself up in love.

Christian leadership done well honors the gifts that each individual has and helps them to develop those gifts beyond what they thought possible. In some ways, Christian leadership is a spark that ignites each of us to recognize and reach our God-given potential while journeying with others. This is how the entire body is edified and how the world is transformed.

Historically, churches and Christian organizations have been a vital part of cultivating future generations of Christian leaders. Through everything from children's plays to youth groups to allowing emerging leaders to participate in worship services and other programs, churches and Christian organizations have offered opportunities to practice leading. These opportunities include preaching and speaking in front of a congregation, organizing service projects, planning special events, working with others to achieve shared priorities, taking leadership positions in ministries, being responsible for completing tasks, and learning how to resolve conflicts. Such opportunities have helped budding leaders to build confidence, hone leadership skills, and learn how to lead others. The key to cultivating Christian leaders is to be deliberate and consistent about making sure there are pathways to support the identification and development of Christian leaders. Ideally, these pathways will help emerging leaders grow and mature in their faith and leadership in ways that go beyond filling in slots to make sure a particular program goes ahead as scheduled. This doesn't necessarily require new programs or ministries, although having intentional leadership training for new and emerging leaders (not just current ones) would be beneficial. There are also ways to integrate leadership training and development into activities that are already planned, including those that are focused on spiritual maturity.

It is also important for Christian leaders to be visionaries—both in fulfilling their assigned tasks and in seeing the gifts, talents, and purpose in the lives of those they're leading. While I recognize that not every leader is gifted as a visionary, I do believe that Christian leaders can be attuned to leading in a way that edifies those they are leading and moves them toward God's purpose for their lives.

Mentoring helps in cultivating Christian leaders because new and emerging leaders are paired with those who have a heart for them and who are concerned about their growth and development. Mentoring does not have to be prearranged or specifically assigned to be effective. Some long-lasting mentoring relationships have happened organically. Having a willingness to be mentored and to mentor others opens the possibilities of cultivating Christian leadership in this way. Mentoring also affords us the opportunity to live in Christian community in a more focused way by devoting time and energy for someone else's benefit. Obviously, special care and attention must be paid to make sure that any mentoring relationship is healthy and devoid of abuse. However, mentoring is a great way to empower and encourage new and emerging leaders emerging leaders to thrive and succeed.

Cultivating Christian leaders happens when it's done on purpose and with purpose. It requires commitment and steadfastness from both the individuals and the institutions to ensure that new and emerging leaders (as well as established leaders) are consistently developing their leadership skills while working to strengthen their faith. Some plant, some water but God gives the increase as it says in 1 Corinthians 3:6 (NKJV). The work of cultivating Christian leaders is holy and necessary. It's an area where many churches and Christian organizations could use some improvement. Certainly, many groups actively and intentionally develop new leaders, while ensuring the ones they have are also growing. However, in too many cases, inconsistent and half-hearted efforts fail to adequately equip and prepare the next generation of Christian leaders to carry on the work of ministry that we have been assigned to do.

Nelson Mandela, the South African leader who eventually became president of the nation. After spending twenty-seven years in prison because he fought against apartheid. He said, "Vision without action is merely a dream. Action without vision just passes the time. Vision with action can change the world."[5] Cultivating Christian leadership is changing and transforming the world. Behold, we are a new creation! Christian leaders—transformational leaders—are tasked with changing the world by doing the hard work of cultivating leadership in one another while tending to it within ourselves.

Notes

1. Ella Baker, "Developing Community Leadership," interview by Gerda Lerner (December 1970), https://americanstudies.yale.edu/sites/default/files/files/baker_leadership.pdf.

2. Ubuntu is a South African proverb. It is defined on the cover of *Believe: The Words and Inspiration of Desmond Tutu* (New York: Blue Mountain Arts, Inc. 2007).

3. John C. Maxwell, *Leadershift: The 11 Essential Changes Every Leader Must Embrace* (Nashville: HarperCollins Leadership, 2019), 216.

4. In Mark 6:8, Jesus orders them to take nothing except a staff. However, this directive is not repeated in the other Gospel accounts.

5. Nelson Mandela, "The Power of Vision" (1991), Joel Arthur Barker https://www.oxfordreference.com/view/10.1093/acref/9780191826719.001.0001/q-oro-ed4-00011987#:~:text=Joel%20Arthur%20Barker%20American%20futurist,action%20can%20change%20the%20world.

Conclusion

"We cannot do everything and there is a sense of liberation in realizing that. This enables us to do something, and to do it very well. It may be incomplete, but it is a beginning, a step along the way, an opportunity for the Lord's grace to enter and do the rest."
—Archbishop Oscar Romero[1]

"Train yourself in godliness, for, while physical training is of some value, godliness is valuable in every way, holding promise for both the present life and the life to come. The saying is sure and worthy of full acceptance. For to this end we toil and struggle, because we have our hope set on the living God, who is the Savior of all people, especially of those who believe. —1 Timothy 4:7b-10

Throughout this book, I have argued that effective and faithful Christian leaders embody Christ-like leadership 24/7, regardless of the setting in which they find themselves leading. We should not be one way at work on a secular job and another way at church or in other Christian contexts. Our leadership grows out of our faith in Christ, and our faith informs our leadership. As I have worked my way through each chapter, I have found myself challenged by my own words. I have wondered out loud if I am being unreasonable or unrealistic. Have I painted an impossible picture for anyone to live up to, including myself?

You may have noticed my wrestling in places where I repeat that I am not talking about Christian leaders being perfect but instead striving to reach a high standard. Often, I have asked myself if I live up to the standards that I have laid out in this work. Am I judging myself by my own words? Perhaps. Then I have reminded myself that although it is a high standard, it is still a standard to strive for in our leadership. As Christian leaders, our standard is Christ, not ourselves or anyone else whom we may admire. First Peter 2:21 says it this way: "For to this you have been called, because Christ also suffered for you, leaving you an example, so that you should follow in his steps." We follow in his steps. We endeavor to grow to be more like him. We work to be transformed into his image and likeness. This is not just what we do as Christian leaders; this is who we are and who we ought to be.

John 7:37-52 records Jesus having an encounter with the crowds and the authorities. He found himself at odds with the religious leaders of the day—again. It was the last day of the Festival of Tabernacles (Booths), a seven-day pilgrimage feast in the fall that marked the end of harvest labor. On this day, Jesus cried out concerning what is really at the heart of what it means to embody Christian leadership. Jesus declared, "As the Scripture has said, 'Out of the believer's heart shall flow rivers of living water'" (John 7:38b). In the end, God is always concerned with our hearts. We confess with our mouths but believe in our hearts. The confession is an outpouring of the belief. Leading as God would have us lead is wrapped up in what flows from our hearts. Living water provides replenishment—nourishment for the soul. Living water provides nutrients, building strength and fortitude, allowing us, as the lyrics from the gospel song sung at my church says, "to run on to see what the end is going to be." Living water gives us joy, peace, patience, and forbearance. I act in love when I want to hate. I am kind when I want to be cruel or callous. I lend a helping hand when I could easily turn my back and walk away. I give when I would much rather receive.

When two hydrogen molecules and one oxygen molecule join, we have water—an amazing transaction that results in transformation. In the same way, belief in Christ, the living water, brings about transformation in our lives. Our transformation then causes a reaction in the world that can transform other people's lives and the communities in which we live: there is a new creation, with the old passing away and everything becoming new (see 2 Corinthians 5:17). We are not the same! Embodying Christ-like leadership means recognizing and operating with the knowledge that being transformed by Christ brings us new life, new hope, and new possibilities for doing greater things than even he did (John 14:12). It empowers us to lead as we're being led and to embody Christ in all that we do. And it fortifies us to withstand the ups and downs, challenges and opportunities, detours, and obstacles that Christian leadership is sure to bring. And so, in parting, I offer this prayer for you and your ministry, in whatever stage of life and in whichever setting you find yourself. Let us pray:

> *Gracious and Merciful God,*
> *We give you thanks for calling us to lead and for showing us how to lead through Christ. We thank you for molding us and shaping us to be more and more like Christ, for keeping us, and for giving us the Holy Spirit to lead us and guide us. We ask, O God, that you would give us clarity of mind and spirit as you help us to navigate the challenges and opportunities that Christian leadership presents. Give us a clean heart and purify us, that our character will withstand the temptations and pitfalls of*

leadership. Strengthen us and give us the courage and conviction we need to lead empowered by you and with authority, humility, and compassion for your people. Reignite in us again and again our commitment to you as if it were the first time we said yes, and prompt us to remember your unceasing and unconditional love for us.

We praise you for your grace and your mercy, which is from everlasting to everlasting and reminds us that we can give our every concern to you, for your yoke is easy and your burden is light. We bless you, O God, for the many ways you care for us even as you urge us to take care of ourselves through sabbath rest and caring for our bodies. We are also mindful of how we must care for one another, and we thank you for the heart and provision to love one another as you have loved us. We pray that you would transform us into the image and likeness of Christ and steer us and guide us away from bad decision-making and poor leadership practices that result in consequences we hope to avoid for ourselves and others. Help us to cultivate other leaders the way you have nurtured us. Grant us your joy, love, and the peace that passes all understanding on this journey, we pray, and bless all those who sojourn with us. May we embody Christ in our leadership, 24/7. In Jesus' matchless name. Amen.

Notes

1. Bishop Ken Untener, "A Prayer of Oscar Romero," November 1979, https://www.bread.org/blog/prayer-oscar-romero.

Selected Bibliography

Barton, Ruth Haley. *Strengthening the Soul of Your Leadership: Seeking God in the Crucible of Ministry*. Downers Grove, IL: InterVarsity Press, 2008.

Brown, Brené. *Dare to Lead: Brave Work. Tough Conversations. Whole Hearts*. New York: Random House, 2018.

Edwards, Tyler. *Zombie Church: Breathing Life Back into the Body of Christ*. Grand Rapids: Kregel Publications, 2011.

Fentress-Williams, Judy. *Holy Imagination: A Literary and Theological Introduction to the Whole Bible*. Nashville: Abingdon Press, 2021.

Greenleaf, Robert. *The Servant as Leader*. Cambridge, MA: Center for Applied Studies, 1970.

——— *The Servant-Leader Within: A Transformative Path*. Hamilton Beazley, Julie Beggs, and Larry C. Spears, eds. Mahwah, NJ: Paulist Press, 2003.

Marsh, Charles. *God's Long Summer: Stories of Faith and Civil Rights*. Princeton, NJ: Princeton University Press, 1999.

Maslansky, Michael with Scott West, Gary DeMoss, and David Saylor. *The Language of Trust: Selling Ideas in a World of Skeptics.* New York: Prentiss Hall Press, 2010.

Maxwell, John C. *Leadershift: The 11 Essential Changes Every Leader Must Embrace.* Nashville: HarperCollins Leadership, 2019.

—— *Leading in Tough Times: Overcome Even the Greatest Challenges with Courage and Confidence.* New York: Center Street, 2021.

McMickle, Marvin A. *The Making of a Preacher: 5 Essentials for Ministers Today.* Valley Forge, PA: Judson Press, 2018.

Nouwen, Henri. *In the Name of Jesus: Reflections on Christian Leadership.* Chestnut Ridge, NY: The Crossroads Publishing Company, 1992.

Palmer, Parker. *Let Your Life Speak: Listening for the Voice of Vocation.* San Francisco: Jossey-Bass, 2000.

Prejean, Helen. "Living My Prayer." *This I Believe II: More Personal Philosophies of Remarkable Men and Women.* Jay Allison and Dan Gediman, eds. New York: Henry Holt & Company, 2008.

Richardson, W. Franklyn. *Witness to Grace: A Testimony of Favor.* Pittsburgh: Church Online, 2020.

Taylor, Barbara Brown. *Leaving Church: A Memoir of Faith.* New York: HarperOne, 2006.

Thurman, Howard. *Meditations of the Heart*. Boston: Beacon Press, 1981.

Walker-Barnes, Chanequa. *Too Heavy a Yoke: Black Women and the Burden of Strength*. Eugene, Oregon: Cascade Books, 2014.

Wolgemuth, Robert. *7 Things You Better Have Nailed Down Before All Hell Breaks Loose*. Nashville: Thomas Nelson, 2008.